The Proud Italians

THE
PROUD ITALIANS

Our Great Civilizers

Carl Pescosolido

Pamela Gleason

National Italian American Foundation

1995

This is the second edition. First edition published by Latium Publishing
Company, in 1991.
International Standard Book Number: 0-9628757-1-6 (cloth)
                                    0-9628757-0-8 (hard cover)
Library of Congress Catalog Card Number: 90-64028

The National Italian American Foundation (NIAF) is the major advocate in Washington, D.C. for the nation's estimated 25 million Italian Americans, the country's fifth largest ethnic group.

Its mission is to help Italian Americans preserve the values of their heritage, and to ensure that the American media and public are aware of the contributions that Italians and their descendants have made to the United States throughout its history. To do this, the NIAF works closely with the Congress and the White House on issues that concern Italian Americans.

Through its many programs, the NIAF also:

- funds cultural and educational conferences
- awards more than $150,000 annually in scholarships
- monitors the media for unflattering stereotyping of Italian Americans and their culture
- works with other Italian-American groups on anti-defamation campaigns

In recent years, the NIAF also has emerged as a critical liaison between Italy and the United States, culturally, politically and economically.

Every year, the NIAF honors outstanding Italians and Italian Americans at its Anniversary Gala Dinner. This event draws nearly 3,000 people from the United States and abroad to Washington, D.C. It has been attended by every sitting American president since 1975.

Past honorees include U.S. Supreme Court Justice Antonin Scalia, Frank Sinatra, Joe DiMaggio, Lee Iacocca, A. Bartlett Giamatti, John Sirica, Liza Minnelli, Luciano Pavarotti, and Sophia Loren.

The NIAF was founded in 1975 as a non-profit, non-partisan foundation legally incorporated in the District of Columbia.

FOR MORE COPIES OF THIS BOOK
OR FURTHER INFORMATION ABOUT NIAF,
PLEASE WRITE:

THE NATIONAL ITALIAN AMERICAN FOUNDATION
1860 19th Street, NW
Washington, DC 20009
(202) 387-0600

Not to know what has happened before we were born is to remain perpetually a child, for what is the worth of human life unless it is woven into the life of our ancestors by the records of history?

-Marcus Tullius Cicero

DEDICATION
by Carl Pescosolido

To my father and mother
who provided me with inspiration
and filled me with pride.

Preface

Carl A. Pescosolido and Pamela Gleason have contributed substantially to informing every student of Western civilization about the prodigious debt that is owed to the Italian people. It is an honor to be invited to compose a preface to their outstanding work.

After discussing the book's contents with "Peski" on several occasions, reading the pre-print and the first edition, I was compelled to present each of my five children with a copy in which I inscribed the following:

> *I present this book to you in the name of my mother and father, and for them, in the name of their mothers and their fathers. It should be a source of inspiration to you and anyone with a name like Ciongoli and to those without a single drop of Italian blood; anyone who has every admired an opera, a classical building, a renaissance painting, the manners of a gentleman, the dignity of an individual or the love of a family.*

To all of you who are about the peruse these pages, I suggest that you read every word, from Harvard professor Richard Tarrant's foreword to the last paragraph in which Cicero admonishes us about the necessity of learning one's history.

A. Kenneth Ciongoli
Senior Vice President
National Italian American Foundation

Contents

Foreword

Most of us have heard Rome called "the Eternal City." Today this title refers to the special place Rome holds in the Catholic church as the seat of the papacy. But it was not the Christians who first described Rome as eternal; the idea arose at the time of the first Roman emperor, Augustus, to express the belief that Rome and its empire would last forever.

The Roman empire no longer holds sway over much of Europe and north Africa - though from Scotland to Libya the Roman presence is vividly recalled by the remains of their roads, temples, and public buildings. In a larger sense, however, the legacy of Rome continues long after its legions and camps have crumbled to dust. The Roman mission was summed up by its greatest poet, Virgil, as the task of "imposing custom on peace" (*paci imponere morem*). This concept implies far more than simply preventing war and maintaining order; it also involves fostering the skills that make up the civilized life of a community, among them laws securing respect for persons and rights, town planning to promote individual comfort and flourishing social exchange, and the pursuit of beauty in art, literature and music. This pattern of a humane civic order was the greatest gift of ancient Rome to its people; it has been constantly renewed by the achievements of Italians over the centuries and now enriches the lives of all of us, whether or not we can claim Italian ancestry.

In this book Carl Pescosolido and Pamela Gleason have documented what we owe the Romans and their Italian descendants. As the subject requires, their treatment ranges widely in time, space and theme: from the mysterious Etruscans to the towering

i

figures of the Renaissance to the scientists, architects, and designers of today. Even readers who have long admired Italy and her past will find much here that is new to them, while for those who may not have reflected on the Italian contribution to our world this book will be an eye-opening experience.

-R.J. Tarrant
Chairman, Department of the Classics
Harvard University

Introduction

I was born in Newton, Massachusetts, to Italian parents. Although at the time when I was growing up, anti-Italian sentiment was rife in the Boston area, I led a sheltered existence. It never occurred to me that anybody would think having Italian roots was anything other than an honor. My father used to tell me stories about great Italian artists and scientists, who became some of my earliest heroes. The only factor that set me apart from my young friends and neighbors was that my last name had five syllables. I remember countless teachers stumbling over it at role call on the first days of school. They would glide easily through the "Arnolds" and the "Jones's", right on to the "Palmers", but at "Pescosolido" they would invariably stop and have to stutter their way through. I was not in the least ashamed of the name, nor of the mispronunciation of it. I used to laugh right along with my classmates.

Although I was always proud of my Italian heritage, I must admit that for most of my life, I was quite ignorant of it. As I grew older, I began to realize that many Americans seemed to consider people of Italian background as somehow inferior to people descended from British or German stock. Worse still, many Italian Americans apparently believed in their inferiority, enough so that some of them actually changed their names to sound more English, while others adopted a defensive attitude. For most of my life, I never thought much about my Italian background one way or another - although Rome, which I visited often, was always my favorite city.

On one of my trips to Rome, however, something happened which was to change completely the way I looked at the world.

[1]

Many people before me have had their lives suddenly alter course in Rome: my experience was by no means unique or original. Strangely enough however, it was not the city itself which brought me to a new way of thinking, nor was it anything or anyone Italian; rather it was Queen Elizabeth of England.

Just by chance I learned that the Queen was in Italy on an official visit and was planning to give a speech at the Italian-parliament. Although I had no idea what to expect from her address, I was curious enough to wrangle myself an invitation. I will never forget the first lines of her speech. Looking out over the Italian crowd, she said "Your ancestors brought civilization to my people."

I don't remember what the rest of the Queen's speech was about - either I was not paying close attention, or I simply forgot, but her opening sentence stuck in my head. I must admit that even though my major in college was history and government, I had never really thought of the Italian people as bringing anything to Britain. I had always simply assumed that each European country developed in its own way, and I had never considered that the Italian people had a particular role in the development of any country other than their own. To the casual listener, what the Queen said might have seemed trivial, but to me, that sentence acted as trigger. From that day on, I was an ardent student of history: I wanted to learn andunderstand as much as I possibly could about the way Italians spread their culture to the peoples of the world.

I read about the Romans and the tremendous Roman Empire, which encompassed all of Europe, the Middle East and Northern Africa. I discovered new things about the Christian religion, which, although it began in the Middle East, took root in Italy and owes its tremendous popularity to the Italians. I rediscovered painting, sculpture, and poetry with the geniuses of the Italian Renaissance, and I learned about the tremendous changes that the Renaissance brought to Europe and to the world. I had always considered Italy to be the most musical land in existence, but it was not until I began to study music that I realized what a huge debt all Western music owes to the Italians, who gave us not simply the greatest composers in the world, but who also invented musical notation and such instruments as the piano, the violin, and the cello. I read about America's founding fathers, and I realized for the first time that they considered Italy to be a land of inspiration, not just in artistic matters, but in philosophical and legal ones as well. In grammar school we learned that the great Italian Columbus discovered America, but I had never been told that *all* of the major early explorations of the New World were led by Italian captains.

I also learned many things which continue to surprise my friends - such as the fact that the city of London, originally called Londinium, was founded and built by Romans long before the Anglo Saxons (who came from Germany) arrived on the British island.

Of course, London is not the only great city built upon Italian foundations. During the second century AD, when the Roman Empire was at its height, practically all of Europe, portions of North Africa, the Middle East, and Southern Russia enjoyed Roman rule, and the Romans left plenty to remember them by. The tremendous monuments, bridges, roads and aqueducts, built two thousand years ago, still inspire awe in tourists to all the countries of the original Roman Empire. Some of these structures lie hidden in the middle of modern cities, like the ancient Cluny baths in Paris's Latin quarter. Others are impossible to overlook, like the huge triple arched aqueduct outside of Nîmes in France. What is so impressive about these Roman remains is that many of them, far from simply surviving through the ages, seem to have triumphed over time itself. Portions of the Nîmes aqueduct are still in working order, and nearby, bull fights are still held in an ancient amphitheater which was once the stage of gladiatorial contests.

Just how advanced was the Roman civilization? It would certainly be an exaggeration to say that the Romans enjoyed all the amenities of modern life, but their standard of living was far higher than most people realize. For instance, even as long ago as 55 BC, some Roman houses were warmed by central heating - a rarity in Paris as recently as 1960. By the third century, it was common for upper class houses in Britain to have glass windows of Roman origin. These windows disappeared with the invasion of the Angles and the Saxons, and were not reintroduced to the island until 1560. The famous Roman roads, leading from Rome to all corners of the Empire, were easily the best in the world until the eighteenth century. Concrete, invented in Rome long before the birth of Chirst, enabled the Romans to build colossal arches which were the mainstay of their architecture. After the decline of Roman power, concrete was virtually forgotten as a building material until the end of the nineteenth century. Most ancient cities were furnished with running water from aqueducts, and many houses had indoor plumbing. A few private homes even sported flush toilets which emptied into the city's elaborate sewer system. The Romans bathed in heated, indoor pools, and their standard of cleanliness was unparalleled in Europe until the nineteenth century. All over the vast Empire, the Romans enjoyed a way of life that was not equaled in comfort for at least fifteen hundred years.

Of course, buildings and roads and baths are not the only things that Rome bequeathed to Europe. Indeed, the Romans left us something far more important than a collection of impressive structures. They spread their laws, their language and the structure of their society to all the people of the western world. The European countries as we know them today grew out of a common, Roman nation, and all of them retain their Roman ancestry. Our systems of law and our forms of government are the direct descendants of Roman laws and governments. Because our modern society sprouted from ancient Roman society, the Roman elements of our culture are totally integrated into daily life. The twelve month, solar based calendar, for instance, was developed by Julius Caesar and revised by Augustus Caesar nearly two thousand years ago. With only minor changes, made by Pope Gregory XIII (another Italian) during the sixteenth century, this is the same calendar we use today: the months of July and August are named after Julius and Augustus, respectively. If we look closely enough, in fact, we can see that many of the things we take for granted in our every day lives actually have Roman or Italian origins.

A large proportion of the words we use today have their roots in ancient Rome. In Europe, the so called "Romance" languages, spoken in France, Spain, Italy, Portugal and Romania are direct descendants of the Latin spoken by Roman legionaries. Even English, though not itself a Romance language, can claim a Latin heritage for about half of its vocabulary. Although Latin is technically considered a "dead" language, its influence is far from being over. Not only do the descendants of Latin make up an important language group, Latin itself continued to be studied and used long after its original speakers disappeared. The Catholic Church used Latin as the language of its liturgy well into the twentieth century and Latin has been the language of learning and scholarship ever since the time of the Roman Empire. Poets and playwrights-composed their verses in Latin throughout the Middle Ages, and many continued to do so even after it became acceptable to write in their own tongues. Scientists, philosophers and mathematicians habitually used Latin to describe their theories and discoveries: for centuries the Roman language was the universal scholarly tongue. Even in America the study of Latin was a major focus of a liberal arts education, where many secondary schools as well as universities actually conducted their classes in Latin until the end of the nineteenth century.

Because Latin was the international scholarly language for so many years, many scientific disciplines still use Latin words and phrases today. The most Roman science of all, the study of law, uses legal terms directly taken from Latin. Some of these terms have found their way into the general English vocabulary. The term *de facto* for instance, is a Latin for "from the fact" while the word *alibi* means, simply "elsewhere." Many non-legal words are also taken directly from Latin: as many as seven hundred English words are unchanged Latin expressions. In addition, some of our most common given names have Latin origins: the names Mark, Peter and Patrick are derived from Roman names, while woman's names such as Amanda, Gloria and Silvia are directly imported from Roman times.

The Romans were the first but by no means the only people from Italy to enrich the culture of the western world. Our Italian heritage has come to us in many different ways. The first way is through the lasting influence of the Roman Empire, which dominated Europe until early in the fifth century. The second way is through Christianity, which became the official Roman state religion during the fourth century and went on to become the most popular religion in the world. Christianity was not, of course, an Italian invention, and, indeed, for over three hundred years, Roman leaders were openly hostile to the Christians, who were viewed as adherents to a dangerous and subversive Jewish sect. Yet, during the fourth century, when Emperor Constantine had a vision and converted, Christianity became a major element of Roman rule. The Romans enforced the spread of the new religion: by the end of the fourth century, all Roman citizens were required to be (or pretend to be) Christian.

As Rome's power declined, the power of Christianity swelled, so that by the fall of the last Emperor, Christianity had taken hold of Europe. The ancient Empire was fragmented politically, but the old Roman territories were unified by a single organized religion. Like the Empire, Christianity was centered in Rome and encompassed all of Europe, as well as England and some northern territories which the Romans never added to their realm, such as eastern Germany, Scandinavia and Ireland. Christianity took the place of the imperial government, providing spiritual and, occasionally, political leadership to the now disparate countries of Europe.

The Church was organized following the Roman model of government, with the Pope as the central authority and other members of the clergy governing each province of the spiritual Empire. Like the Roman generals who reported back to the Emperor, Christian bishops reported back to the Pope. During the Middle Ages, the Church was the wealthiest and most important power in all of Europe, and the Pope was often the most powerful person in the European political as well as religious spectrum. Kings deferred to him, and wars were fought only with his blessing. Thus the Church, like the ancient Empire, inspired Europe to look to Italy for guidance in political, military and personal matters.

Christianity remained intimately connected to Rome throughout the long Middle Ages and into the Renaissance. Because of this deep bond with Italy, Christianity is responsible for disseminating many elements of Italian culture throughout the world. The Catholic Church used and preserved Latin texts and some of the techniques of Roman art and architecture, thus ensuring their survival into a later epoch. Other elements of Christian worship retained a distinctly Italian character. Church music, for instance, which was similar throughout the Christian realm, was essentially

[6]

Italian music. A British Christian of the tenth century might sing Latin hymns composed by Italian monks. He might worship in a church filled with paintings inspired by Italian frescoes. The great majority of Europeans in the Middle Ages were Christians, and Christianity, with its ethical and moral code based on Roman models, shaped the minds not just of the common citizens, but of the writers, artists and rulers as well.

Christianity continued to dominate the cultural development of the Western world throughout the Middle Ages and into the new and exciting period known as the Renaissance, when Italian ideas and ideals swept dramatically across Europe, reviving and revitalizing every culture they contacted. The Renaissance, which officially began during the fifteenth century but has its roots deep in the Middle Ages, was a tremendous artistic, philosophical and scientific movement which first blossomed in Florence and then sent its seeds northward into Europe. The term Renaissance is French for rebirth, and refers to the renewal of interest in classical Roman and Greek styles of art, architecture and literature. A time of tremendous progress and productivity in the arts, the Renaissance was a period of discovery and rediscovery. Ancient Roman authors, whose works were ignored and practically lost for centuries suddenly found a wide readership. Stirred by the ancients, contemporary poets found new voices and began to write movingly and personally in their native tongues. Ancient Roman and Greek sculptures and frescoes awakened artistic impulses in stone-cutters and painters, while ancient monuments inspired architects to create splendid palaces and cathedrals. The Renaissance spirit spread outward from Italy and eventually affected the greater part of Europe.

Although the Renaissance provoked imitation of the ancient Romans, the Italian contribution was not limited to providing the world with ancient models. The greatest creative minds of that (and arguably of any) time came out of Renaissance Italy. Leonardo Da Vinci, Michelangelo, Botticelli, Raphael and scores of other brilliant Italian artists created some of the most magnificent and stirring paintings, sculptures and buildings the world has ever seen. Dante, Petrarch, and Boccaccio, the greatest Italian writers, breathed new life into the literary world, inspiring such authors as

[7]

Rabelais, Shakespeare and Milton. The movable type printing press was invented in Germany, and printing houses, such as the Aldine Press in Venice began turning out volumes of the classics and of contemporary works which large numbers of people could afford. The world was reading again, and the attainment of knowledge became, once again, a noble pursuit.

The inquisitive attitude of Renaissance Italy opened a door into the creative soul of humankind. A new spirit of energy and curiosity quickened the pulse of Europe, and everywhere people began to investigate the world in which they lived. It was a time of tremendous discovery. During the Renaissance, Christopher Columbus, who sailed under a Spanish flag, but was an Italian born in Genoa, landed in the new world. Columbus's courage and vision exemplify the bold spirit of the Italian Renaissance, and his achievement in discovering two huge continents ranks him among the most important people in the history of the world. While the credit for discovering the New World goes deservedly to Columbus, another Italian, a Florentine navigator named Amerigo Vespucci, earned the honor of having his name affixed to the new lands as they were drawn on the map, after proving that they were indeed new continents and not the outer islands of China and the Far East.

While Columbus and Vespucci surveyed the contours of the globe, Renaissance scientists, writers and artists looked inward to examine the intricacies of human anatomy and physiology. Leonardo da Vinci, perhaps one of the most versatile artists in our history, drew the internal structures of the human body so accurately and so precisely his drawings have been compared to xray photos. Petrarch, whose poetry inspired all of Europe, wrote honestly about love, hope and the human condition. The pioneers of the Renaissance discovered new continents, new forms of expression and new facts about the physical and spiritual world.

The Renaissance was a worldly rather than a religious age. The Catholic Church, which monopolized the best minds of the Middle Ages, was too restrictive for the Renaissance thinker. Scholars and artists began to occupy themselves with human affairs, openly delighting in earthly things. The philosophy known as humanism was born. The humanists studied the classics - great men, great art, and great ideas - seeking worldly, rather than strictly religious enlightenment. Humanist thinkers sought the perfection of the human being as well as an understanding of the workings of the natural world. They did not turn away from God, but rather looked for the divine in all things. Italian humanist philosophy spread northward, bringing with it a new celebration of the individual which shaped our modern understanding of the goals of human existence.

From the Renaissance onward, Italy has inspired countless people throughout the world. After the end of the Renaissance movement, Europeans continued to look to Italy for their cultural and intellectual educations. During the eighteenth century, the age of the so-called Grand Tour, thousands of British, European and American people made pilgrimages to Italy, not simply to study her great artists and writers, but to learn something of the refined manners and style of the Italian people. Italy was not only a place of tremendous achievement, it was also extremely fashionable. An Englishman, after completing the Grand Tour, which usually entailed extended visits to Florence, Rome, Venice and Naples, would return to his native land, bringing back a taste for Italian art, clothing, landscape and music. Opera, born in Italy, swept through Europe, bringing with it ornate, Italian inspired opera houses. Homes and gardens in France and England were redesigned to resemble Italian villas and *giardini*. Italy was considered a land of culture, and Italian trends, whether in art, architecture, music, manners or fashion, set the style for Europe and ultimately for America.

America itself owes Italy a great debt. All of the major European explorations of the new continent were led by Italian captains, from Columbus and Vespucci to Verrazzano and John Cabot. Cabot, of course, was really named Giovanni Cabotto, and, although he sailed for the English, he was born in Genoa and had lived in Venice before he relocated his family to England in order to serve King Henry VII. Although Italy set up no colonies on American shores, she did send plenty of citizens, both in colonial times and over the ensuing centuries. Italian thinkers and writers helped to crystallize the thoughts of such men as Jefferson and Adams, while Italian artisans labored to construct monuments worthy of the new country. Italy, and her Roman past, inspired the physical architecture of America's government as well as its philosophical structure. Like Ancient Rome, Washington DC is centered around a Capitol, and is presided over by the Senate. It is no accident that the buildings of our nation's capital resemble Roman monuments. Ancient Rome was a role model for our country.

Italy continued to contribute more than her share to the advancement of our culture from the age of the Grand Tour until the present day. Despite centuries of political strife, foreign domination and the resultant economic hardship, Italy still managed to give us some of the most important innovations of modern life. The wireless telegraph and the microwave, for instance, were invented by the Italian Gugliemo Marconi, a brilliant scientist from Bologna. The nuclear age was ushered in by Enrico Fermi, a physicist from Rome, who was the first to successfully split the atom and whose discoveries led to the creation of the atomic bomb and the end of World War II. Other Italian inventors include Antonio Meucci, who created the first working telephone several years before Alexander Graham Bell. Sadly, Meucci, who lived in the United States, never got the credit for his invention (called the telettrophone), and died penniless.

Because Italy suffered from political fragmentation and economic woes from the days of the Renaissance well into the twentieth century, many Italians left their native country to seek better fortunes in Europe, England and especially in North and South America. Italian immigrants make up the fourth largest ethnic group in North America. While many first generation immigrants who came to this country at the end of the nineteenth and the first half of the twentieth century were relatively poor and uneducated, they shared a common sense of strong family values and dedication to hard work that enabled many of their sons and daughters to become some of the most prominent and respected people in our country. They are doctors, lawyers, judges, teachers, businessmen and inspiring political leaders.

Hard work and commitment to family significantly raised the living standard of the average Italian American. While half a century ago, many Italian Americans were below the poverty line, today Italian Americans are significantly better off and better

[10]

educated than most non-Italians. In fact, the income level of Italian Americans is almost fifteen percent above the national average, while business ownership is seventy percent higher among Italian Americans than among the rest of the nation. Even in these changing times, family stability is still highly prized by the Italians: almost ninety eight percent of Italian Americans live in a family situation, and Italians are far less likely than other Americans to put aged people in nursing homes.

Back in Europe, the same strong values have pulled Italy out of a financial abyss and onto the world stage both in terms of economic output and in terms of the quality of Italian made products. The gross national product of Italy today is fourth in the world, behind the United States, Japan and Germany but ahead of England and France. Italians are among the thriftiest people in the world, with a household savings rate exceeding that of even the Japanese. Italian products, from Gucci shoes to the unequaled Ferrari automobile are among the most highly sought after and respected goods in the world. Major Italian corporations are also among the largest in the world, from Fiat, the giant automobile company, to Olivetti, which went from making typewriters to manufacturing computers and remains one of Eurpoe's most successful companies. Neither is Italy a stingy country: Italians are the world's fifth largest foreign aid donors, giving out over four billion dollars annually to victims of natural and man-made disasters.

Given Italy's new-found prosperity and long history of cultural preeminance, it is no wonder that Italy is once again becoming fashionable. Italian food, for instance, has gained international stature and reputation. Some of the fanciest and most expensive restaurants in America now serve and even specialize in Italian cuisine. The simpler foods of Italy have also found world-wide acceptance. What family in America does not keep a box of spaghetti in the cupboard, and what American city is there where one cannot get a pizza? It was not long ago that Italian foods were difficult to come by. Now even exotic Italian ingredients can be purchased in most supermarkets, especially in big cities. Not only are Italian foods available, but the latest medical advice advocates eating more of such Italian staples as pasta, and there is even

[11]

evidence that a small daily ration of olive oil might help prevent heart disease.

One thing that has always impressed me about the Italian people is their innate and superb sense of style. This style is reflected in their art, their clothing, their automobiles, their use of language and even their furniture. Italian style seems to be connected with the Italian appreciation for and love of beauty. This love of beauty can be traced back thousands of years to the Romans and to the Etruscans before them. Italian design, from the Roman Pantheon, built in the year 124, to the Ferrari Testarossa of 1994, takes beauty as its ultimate goal, and Italian products are as beautiful as they are functional. It is no wonder then, that Italian clothing has taken over the international market. Milan is poised to overtake Paris as the fashion capital of the world, and Italian based chain stores selling Italian made clothing can be found all over Europe, Asia, Australia and the Americas.

In many ways, a Western heritage is an Italian heritage. From the Romans to Christopher Columbus, on down to the fashion designers of the 1990's, Italian people have a long tradition of cultural leadership. Over these past years, I have studied our Italian roots almost constantly, and I am continually amazed by the depth, breadth and diversity of Italian contributions to our world. Every day, it seems, I learn of a new way in which Italian influences have shaped, and continue to shape our lives. Appreciation for Italy is also on the rise, nowhere more so than in the United States, where Italian Americans are only now beginning to take stock of their own rich culture.

The first edition of this book met with such a resounding welcome that it became clear that a new edition would be necessary. Much of the material on these pages comes directly out of the history books or newspaper and magazine articles. Although some of the facts in this book will surely be well known to the reader, we think that this book will contain many revelations for the average American. I am especially proud that the National Italian American Foundation has chosen to publish the book for distribution to its members, because I believe that understanding our history is the first step in improving our present and bettering our future.

I hope that people of Italian descent will take a special interest in what we have to say, but I think that all people, whatever their background, should feel a sense of pride in the achievements of our Italian ancestors. Great men and great ideas have no nationality: the visions of a Leonardo Da Vinci, the courage of a Christopher Columbus and the genius of a Guglielmo Marconi belong to the whole human race, not just to the Italian people. One of the greatest discoveries I have made in the course of my studies is the unity of all humankind. We should all be inspired by the stupendous attainments of the Italian people, because wherever our parents were born, we have all been enriched by them. In a sense, we are all Italians.

July 14, 1994
Carl A Pescosolido

The Lion Columns in Ravello, Italy

CHAPTER ONE:

All Roads Lead To Rome

The year is 130 AD, Emperor Hadrian stands at the helm of the greatest Empire ever known, and all roads lead to Rome. They travel in straight lines, cutting through hills and uneven territory, traversing streams and brooks and rivers from Northern England to Northern Africa, from Western Spain to Western Russia. Everywhere the roads lead, they show us more evidence of the greatness of Roman civilization. They bring us to splendid libraries, parks and amphitheaters on the edge of African deserts. They take us to the south of France, where every day an enormous aqueduct transports thirty one million gallons of water from its source to a city thirty miles away. They carry us northward, through the rains and fogs of England, to a great wall, seventy three miles long, ten feet wide and fifteen feet high, which marks the boundary of the civilized world. Everywhere the roads lead, we also find people who call themselves Romans; people who are proud to be a part of this great and unified Empire, and who speak the Latin language which has spread throughout the realm. Indeed, it is incorrect to say that all roads lead to Rome, because in reality, all roads are in Rome. In 130 AD, Rome is far more than just the city which founded the great Empire, it is the Empire itself. Everywhere we go, if we were to ask the people about their nationality, we would hear the statement *civis romanus sum*: I am a Roman citizen.

We have started with the year 130 AD, because it stands in the

[15]

middle of what was the most peaceful and creative period in Roman history. It was also a time when the Roman Empire had its largest physical size. From 117 AD until the end of the second century, the Empire covered over 1.3 million square miles, and some estimates put its population at close to one hundred million people. If we were to compare a modern map of Europe with one from 130 AD, we would see that during the reign of Hadrian, over thirty modern European, Mid-Eastern and African countries were provinces of the Empire. All of these now separate modern countries once existed peacefully, united by the laws, government and language of their Roman civilizers. Although the different provinces themselves each retained something of their own individual flavor, all of Europe, the Middle East and North Africa was unified and whole under Roman law.

It may be difficult for us to imagine all of these now separate and distinct countries obeying the laws of one government; it is perhaps even more difficult for us to imagine the climate of peace in the realm. For nearly two hundred years, the Roman Empire governed its territories without any major wars. Each province was protected by a strong and well organized military which discouraged hostile forces. By the second century AD, the Roman army had subdued just about every population it had come into contact with. The self-confident Roman people considered themselves the rulers of the world. They had achieved what seems next to impossible today: a lasting world peace. This period of peace, which began with the reign of the Emperor Augustus in 27 BC and lasted until the death of Emperor Marcus Aurelius in 180 AD, is known as the *pax romana* or Roman peace. Some historians, such as Edward Gibbon, consider the two centuries of the pax romana to be the most fruitful period in human history. Gibbon, whose famous history, *The Decline and Fall of The Roman Empire*, was long considered the authority on Roman civilization, said that the pax romana was "the period in the history of the world during which the human race was the most happy and prosperous."

Of course, never in the history of the world have happiness and prosperity been shared equally by everybody. The pax romana, likewise, could hardly have been a happy or a pacific time for the unlucky residents of those provinces that did have quarrels with Roman rule. Numerous uprisings took place in Germany, where war-like tribes chafed under foreign domination. Britain was captured during the time of the pax romana. Although the Roman army had little trouble appropriating the island's lowlands, the conquest was certainly not a bloodless one, and it took nearly thirty years of intermittent fighting to vanquish the wilder tribes in the hills of Wales. All was still not quiet after Britain's capture: in the year 60 AD, the famous British Queen Boudicca lead a bloody revolt against the Romans. The uprising was squashed, but only after it cost the Empire a reported seventy thousand lives. Residents of Masada in the Judaean desert would probably not have many good things to say about the Roman Empire or about the pax romana. Masada, which was a natural hill fortress, was the last Jewish stronghold against the Romans. Roman legions besieged the town in 73 AD, and managed to break through the walls. Rather than be captured by the Romans, the residents of Masada - 960 men, women, and children - burnt their possessions and committed suicide.

All of these unfortunate events took place during the first century of Roman peace. While the first century of the pax romana was troubled by occasional power struggles and uprisings throughout the realm, the second half of the pax romana was much more tranquil. By the end of the first century, the Roman Empire had evolved into an orderly and smooth-running system. Emperors were proud of being able to maintain peace throughout the realm, and the idea of harmony was treasured by Roman citizens. Contemporary writers are at least partly responsible for the historical perception that the Romans brought peace to the land. The Romans liked to promote the idea that their rule had forever abolished war. In the words of one subject writing during the second century AD:

> The whole world keeps holiday; the age-long curse of war has been put aside; mankind turns to enjoy happiness. Strife has been quieted, leaving only the competition of cities, each eager to be the most beautiful and the most fair. Every city is full of gymnastic schools, fountains and porticos, temples, shops, and schools of learning. The whole earth is decked with beauty like a garden.

[17]

Although this description is perhaps too idyllic to be believed entirely, the stability of the Roman government did provide its citizens with a kind of security that the world had never known before and Europe has never known since. Because of this stability, subjects of Rome could focus their energies on improving the quality of their lives, rather than on simply surviving.

One of the reasons that the Romans were able to administer their Empire so successfully was that they learned to adapt themselves to the different parts of the world which they ruled. Instead of uniformly imposing Roman law and Roman leaders on all of the cities of the Empire, the Romans incorporated local laws and local people within the framework of their government. By doing this, the Romans gave the common people all over the Empire a sense of sharing in its fortunes. The people in the provinces were willing to make sacrifices for the good of the Empire, and for the most part did not resist the laws and government of the Roman people. Over time, as the Empire became established, people no longer saw the Romans as a foreign power, but instead saw themselves as Romans. In the early years of Roman rule, all of the people in the provinces were not granted full Roman citizenship, but to be a Roman citizen was the highest honor to which a provincial could aspire. Provincials could become citizens through community or military service, or if the city they lived in became an official Roman colony. As time wore on, the Empire granted citizenship more and more freely, and by the third century, virtually all free subjects of Rome were citizens. Rome understood that an Empire made up of loyal citizens was far superior to an Empire composed of stern rulers and beleaguered subjects.

In fact, flexibility was the most distinctive trademark of the Roman way of operating. It has often been said that the Romans did not create the things which made their culture so rich; they simply borrowed them from the people they conquered. While this statement is partially true, it is important to realize that the word "simply" is misleading. In the first place, the Romans improved on most of the things that they found in other cultures, and did not just copy them wholesale. In the second place, in order to be able to successfully "borrow" ideas, building methods, literary and artistic forms and so on, the Romans needed to be open-minded

[18]

and willing to learn. When the Romans conquered Greece, they did not simply destroy Grecian culture the way barbarian tribes would later on; instead, they learned from the Greeks and so enriched themselves. Although they were not exempt from a certain amount of chauvinism, the Romans did not turn up their noses at foreign accomplishments. When they saw something they liked in a foreign culture, they adopted it as their own.

The atmosphere of tolerance fostered by Roman rule created an excellent environment for artists and artisans as well as for literary and scientific minds. Because the Romans were able to adapt and adopt things from other cultures and use them within their own highly organized framework, Roman artistic and utilitarian achievements reached a level not seen before in the ancient world. From the Etruscans, early leaders of ancient Italy, the Romans learned how to use arches and domes to build tall structures. From the Phoenician and Greek settlers in the southern parts of Italy, they learned the principles of making concrete, a material which they improved and then used to fortify their aqueducts, amphitheaters and bath houses. As the Empire expanded, the Romans spread their well-built and well-engineered structures from Italy to Africa, the Middle East and Europe. Not only were these works of Roman engineering and architecture impressive to look at, they also considerably raised the standard of living in the ancient world. Indoor plumbing, hot and cold running water, central heating, and lighted streets were all available in some Roman cities. The Romans did not merely conquer people of the Empire; they brought them the real, palpable advantages of civilization. The true Roman genius lay in the construction of things which served important and valuable purposes.

Perhaps the best example of Roman practical genius are the legendary Roman roads which connected all of the cities within the vast Empire. Of course the Romans were not the first people to build roads: from the beginning of civilization, people have constructed roads to make it easier to get from one place to the next. Roman roads were not even the first to be built in Italy; the Greeks in the south and the Etruscans in the north had road systems even before Rome was established as a city. But the Roman roads were significantly different from and considerably better than any roads or road systems ever invented. Roman roads were paved, straight, broad, level, and flat, and they could cut across swampy ground and mountainous territory with equal ease. They were meticulously designed by surveyors and engineers, and they were so well built that many of them survive even today. Originally, the Romans made their roads so that the army could travel more easily to the distant provinces, but the roads soon became valuable lifelines for civilians as well.

The roads built by Rome can, in fact, be seen as a kind of a symbol for Roman civilization itself. They were well planned, carefully constructed, and constantly maintained both by the original Romans who built them, and by the new Romans whose lands they travelled through. Straight and true, they stand for the principles of honesty and justice which the Roman culture believed in. Adapting to all landscapes, they were equally at home in the deserts of Northern Africa, the mountainous regions of France and Spain, and the marshy lowlands of Belgium and Holland. They showed that these different regions of the world could be united under one system, and they proved that Rome was able to overcome natural and cultural boundaries and bring civilization to all of the people of the Empire. Of course, like the roads themselves, the Roman Empire was difficult to establish and laborious to maintain. The Romans were well organized, brilliant administrators, but they were not superhuman. The difficulty of creating and preserving such a vast Empire cannot be over emphasized.

To begin to comprehend the size and achievements of ancient Rome, perhaps we should take a trip down some of these roads and see where they lead us. The Roman Empire was so vast and its cities and monuments so numerous, our trip will necessarily be an abbreviated one. It would take many thousands of pages to bring the entire Roman Empire to life, so instead, we shall sample cities in some of the major provinces of the Empire. A logical place for us to begin would be, of course, in the city of Rome itself, where all the major roads converge at one point; The Golden Milestone which stands beside the Temple of Saturn in the center of the Roman Forum.

We began this chapter with the old saying "All roads lead to Rome." Here, the Golden Milestone, a tall column erected by the

Emperor Augustus in 20 BC, is the point to which these roads lead. The distances from Rome to all the major cities in the Empire were marked on the column with gilt bronze letters. During Rome's early years, the Forum was the commercial, religious and political heart of the city, where shops shared space with government buildings and temples, and the open spaces teemed with Romans from all walks of life. Although when Rome became an Empire, the Forum ceased to be a political center, it remained an important monumental area, and its buildings - which are now only ruins - were once quite splendid indeed. The Forum once held the Senate building, temples built to Saturn, Jupiter, Concord, Vespasian, the Deified Caesar, and Castor and Pollux. The Forum also housed the Vestal Virgins, triumphal arches, basilicas, and the State archives, as well as fountains and bronze statues of the twelve Olympian gods. The many buildings of the Forum were once covered with gleaming, multi-colored marble, some brought from Italian quarries, some imported from far away provinces of the Empire.

The function of the Forum was not strictly religious or monumental, however. Here, merchants sold everything from food and medicine to make-up, clothing and jewelry; orators and politician argued about current affairs, religious processions passed down the *via sacra*, and ordinary men, women, and children strolled in the sunshine. Rome was home for about a million people of widely varied wealth and social class. In the Forum one might encounter beggars and prostitutes, as well as priests, lawyers, fortune tellers, soldiers, slaves and wealthy cosmopolitan women on their way to the baths. Because Rome was the center of the ancient world, one could also expect to see many exotic people from distant lands. By the second century AD, the people of Rome were quite accustomed to imported goods and foreigners hawking their wares. Oriental spices and fabrics were quite popular. Brightly colored birds from Africa could be had at moderate prices. The fashion industry was alive and well: Roman women might buy imported kohl eyeliner from Egyptian merchants, or a blonde wig, made from the hair of a German slave girl.

The Forum, like all of Rome, was for pedestrians only. The city's roads were too narrow and winding for the volume of traffic which began to flow down them as Rome's size and importance grew. Accordingly, during the first century BC, Julius Caesar passed a law outlawing chariot traffic within city limits during daylight hours. After dark, the restriction was lifted so that wagons could bring deliveries to stores or building materials to works in progress. Today in Rome, as in many other cities of Europe and America, certain sections are reverting back to the ancient "pedestrians only" rule. Perhaps, after sitting hours in a traffic jams on a narrow and congested streets, listening to the symphony of honking horns and breathing exhaust fumes, today's Romans are coming to realize that their ancestors had the right idea in the first place.

From the Forum, one can see the Colosseum, the largest and most important amphitheater of the Empire. A one hundred foot high gilt bronze statue of a man, called the Colossus, once stood beside it, and smaller statues once filled the archways in its walls. Built in the first century A.D., the Colosseum covers six acres and had seating accommodations for fifty thousand spectators. The building was so well planned and its eighty entrances were so well arranged, the entire audience could be cleared from it in ten minutes. Spectators sat in comfort, protected from the hot sun by an enormous awning which could be drawn across the top of the building like a roof. The shows which took place inside the theater frequently involved wild animals, which were kept in cages underneath the arena floor. The cages, lifted with pulleys, could be brought up through trap doors to appear at the appropriate moment. The Colosseum is still standing today, but the precious marble which once lined its interior walls, like the marble which once covered the monuments of the Forum, is gone. While some of the marble was shaken off by earthquakes during the thirteenth and fourteenth centuries, most of it was actually stolen to build splendid new Christian churches during the Renaissance.

Nowadays, the most prominent structure which one can see from the Colosseum is the triumphal Arch of Constantine. In 130 AD, however, this arch had not yet been erected. Instead, the Colosseum was surrounded by other monumental buildings, like the Temple of Venus and Rome which was constructed by Hadrian. Nearby, a marble fountain, richly adorned with statues, testified to the Roman love for moving water. The fountain, called the *meta sudans*, was shaped like one of the turning points around which chariots raced in the most famous race track in the world, the Circus Maximus.

The Circus Maximus was not far from the Colosseum. It was a tremendous, oval track, with enough seats for three hundred thousand people. From these seats, spectators usually watched chariot races, although occasionally hunts or mock battles would be staged instead. In the center of the track ran a long and narrow barrier called the *spina*, which was decorated with various statues, obelisks, fountains and two small temples. Chariot races generally required the competitors to complete seven laps of track, and spectators could keep count of how many laps had been run by watching the tops of the temples, one of which was equipped with seven large marble eggs, the other with seven marble dolphins. Each time the chariots completed a lap, one of the dolphins and one of the eggs would be removed from the top of the building, until, with the seventh lap, all of the objects were gone.

Perhaps the most famous building in Rome is the Pantheon which was started in 27 BC under Emperor Augustus and rebuilt by Emperor Hadrian around 120-124 AD. The Pantheon was originally constructed as a temple to worship all of the pagan gods in Rome. After Christianity became the state religion, the temple was re-dedicated to the Virgin Mary, and became an active Catholic church. Essentially perfectly preserved, the Pantheon has been used as a place of worship continuously for two thousand years. Its state of preservation, its great size and its pleasingly decorated interior make it hard for many visitors to believe how old it really is. The dome which makes up its roof is one hundred and forty two feet in diameter and one hundred and forty two feet high. A circular hole, thirty feet across, is cut out of the top of the dome, and the light which comes down into the building illuminates the interior, and invites worshippers to contemplate the heavens. At the time it was made, the Pantheon had the largest poured concrete dome in the world. In fact, today, it still does.

The Emperor Hadrian, whose Pantheon is so universally admired, is a good example of the well-rounded genius of the Roman people. Not only was he a brilliant leader and the ruler of Rome for twenty years, he was also a seasoned traveler and a practicing architect. Along with the Emperors Augustus and Marcus Aurelius, he was also among the few Roman Emperors who was remembered as a poet. Hadrian knew his vast Empire quite well. During the first years of his reign, he journeyed throughout the provinces, mostly on foot. On his travels, he planned and oversaw the construction of cities, temples, baths and other buildings. His most famous achievement is probably Hadrian's Wall, a huge barrier built to protect northern Britain from wild Scottish tribes. However, Hadrian's accomplishments go far beyond mere wall-building. He was a learned and a cultured man, who displayed the particularly Roman ability to appreciate, imitate and improve upon the native art and architecture he found in the various provinces.

We do not have to travel far from Rome to see a large sample of Hadrian's versatile architectural skill. Following the *via Tiburtina* to the east, we come to Tivoli, Hadrian's own villa. Calling Tivoli a "villa" is perhaps a bit misleading: Hadrian built himself a vast estate, covering enough land and including enough buildings to qualify as a city in itself. Hadrian continued to add to Tivoli until the end of his life, and the villa incorporates original architectural styles inspired by all the places he visited. Temples reminiscent of Athens and statues like those found in the Nile Delta mingle with traditional Roman vaulted bath houses, swimming pools and fountains. Tivoli is still being excavated, and archaeologists esti mate that the original villa was five times the size of the section that has been unearthed today.

Although we have barely glanced at the Roman works in and around the capital, it is time to move on to the Roman provinces. We shall follow a road out of the city and into the greater world of the ancient Empire. Many thousands of Roman citizens and military men once marched these roads, and they lead to all corners of the ancient world. From Rome, we move northward on the *via Flaminia* to Verona, which lies at the foot of the Alps. Verona, which became a Roman colony in 89 BC, was important because it lay at the junction of several main roads between Italy and Northern Europe. Famous today as the setting for Shakespeare's *Romeo and Juliet*, Verona was one of many large Roman towns in Italy. A fortified city, Verona was surrounded by high walls

View of the Colosseum from the Roman Forum

The Roman *Pont du Gard* in Nîmes, France

Statue at Tivoli, Hadrian's Villa

(portions of which are still standing today) and had a large theater as well as an amphitheater. The amphitheater is still used today for open air operatic performances.

From Verona, we travel northwards on the *via Claudia Augusta*, a broad and an inviting road which takes us through the Resia Pass, across the Alps and into the Roman Province of Raetia. The capital of this province, Augusta Vindelicum, is now called Augsburg, and stands in the middle of what is now southern Germany. In Roman times, Raetia was not particularly noteworthy from a cultural point of view, but it was important economically for its native stores of tin, and strategically as a German outpost of the Empire. Throughout their history, the Romans had trouble dominating Germanic peoples. Numerous Roman leaders tried to expand their territory into German lands, but with little success. Germanic tribes were known to be fierce in battle and little inclined to become subjects of the Romans. The Germanic peoples' independent nature, coupled with the densely forested and mountainous terrain which they inhabited, accounts for the fact that Roman presence in central and northern Germany was never more than minimal. Not only did the Romans find the Germanic warriors fierce adversaries, they were also daunted by the cold, damp German climate. For all their ambition, the Romans were, in the end, just as happy not to occupy such an inhospitable country. They were, however, quite anxious to guard their pleasant provinces from Northern hostility: the ancient tribes of Germania were well known for expansionist tendencies. Raetia, while it did not have a tremendous cultural impact on the Empire, did offer Rome a Germanic stronghold.

Augusta Vindelicum lay near the Danube river, which, for many years, was one of the boundaries of the Empire. Following the river to the east, we pass through the province of Noricum, which is now Austria, and, from there, we move into the larger province of Pannonia which covers most of present day Hungary. Pannonia was far more important to the Empire than either Raetia or Noricum, and for this reason had a more highly developed Roman civilization.Pannonia connected the eastern and the western halves of the Empire. Without control of Pannonia, the east and the west would have been cut off from overland communication.

Furthermore, if some other nation were to capture Pannonia, the city of Rome itself would be vulnerable to attack. Because of the province's strategic significance, the Romans deployed more sol diers to Pannonia than to any other peaceful part of the Empire. During the second century, the one hundred and fifty mile stretch of the Danube between present day Austria and present day Budapest was guarded by four Roman legions, each of which was made up of about five thousand soldiers. Obviously, those soldiers needed to have somewhere to live, and so they built cities.

One of the military cities which sprang up along the Danube to house the Roman legionaries was called Aquincum. Actually, Aquincum was a city long before the Romans got to Pannonia. Its name probably came from the ancient, Celtic name of the city, "Ak-ink" which meant "good waters." Ak-ink was situated on the banks of the Danube, where many natural springs supplied the natives with hot and cold water, much of it laden with iron, sulfur and other supposedly health-restoring minerals. When the Romans came to Ak-ink, they first built a camp for the soldiers, but within a short time, a civilian city grew up as well.

Like most Roman cities, Aquincum was well-planned. The land was surveyed and analyzed by professional city planners. All of the streets were laid out in an orderly fashion, and all of them were made straight and at right angles to each other. While the surveyors and engineers established the street plan, other professionals constructed sewers and an aqueduct, which would transport enough water to provide all of the inhabitants with a plentiful supply. Places of entertainment were planned and built nearby. Space was allotted for park and agricultural use. Empty areas were reserved within the city walls to allow for the natural growth of the population. Over the years, the city grew up neatly and efficiently, with none of the cramped or overcrowded conditions which unplanned cities are subject to.

The houses of Aquincum were made of stone, and decorated in the Roman way, with mosaic floors and painted walls. Although the city was originally built by people who had come from Rome itself, they soon intermingled with the Celts who had founded Ak-Ink. The Celtic inhabitants of Aquincum enjoyed the privileges and civilized lifestyle of Rome, and the fabled good waters and hot springs which they, and their ancestors, had always possessed. Today, Aquincum is a part of Budapest, capital of Hungary, and the remains of the ancient Roman town, its baths, aqueduct, amphitheaters, and even its houses, are very much visible. New Roman remains are being discovered almost every day, both because of the expansion of the city and through systematic excavation. One of the most satisfying outdoor museums of Roman ruins anywhere is actually in and around a Budapest subway station, where parts of an old road and the gate to the city have been uncovered, along with monuments, statues and a military bath house.

To the east of Pannonia, lay the province of Dacia, where now we have Romania and the Ukraine. Dacia was prized for its rich silver, iron and gold mines. The last province to be annexed to the Empire, Dacia was captured in 106 AD by the Emperor Trajan, who immediately began to set up colonies and build roads. Ruins of Roman bridges and walls can be found throughout the province, and Roman inscriptions have been discovered even in remote mountainous regions. Although by their own standards, the Romans only ruled Dacia for a short time (one hundred and sixty three years), nonetheless, Rome made a tremendous impact on the province. Many modern day Romanians consider themselves descendants of the ancient Romans. Not only does the name "Romania" refer to Rome, but the Romanian language is also, like French and Spanish, a romance language.

Just south of Dacia lay the provinces of Moesia and Thrace, where now we have Bulgaria, and west of these, bordering the Adriatic sea, was Dalmatia in the former Yugoslavia. The third century Emperor Diocletian was probably born in Salona, the ancient capital of Dalmatia. When he retired from the throne, he returned to the area, building himself a large palace in a suburb called Spalato. Diocletian's palace was laid out like a Roman military camp and built on a grand scale. During the Middle Ages, an entire town grew up within its walls, and eventually, the city spilled over its ancient boundaries. In modern times, Diocletian's retreat became Split, a large and important city in the former Yugoslavia, famous for its deep, safe harbor, which was known as the finest on the Adriatic coast. Many Roman remains, such as the walls which once surrounded the city and Diocletian's mausoleum, remain present and visible.

Moving southward along the Adriatic coast, the next Roman province was Macedonia, followed by Epirus and Achaia, which are now Albania and Greece. One does not usually think of the Romans as the rulers of Greece. People like to think that the Greeks were entirely separate from the Romans, and that, while Greek culture influenced Roman culture, the Romans did not give anything back to Greece. However, this popular conception is not entirely correct. The Golden Age of Greece came before the Golden Ages of Rome, and therefore, the Romans, who were always ready to learn from other cultures, learned from, and were inspired by the Greeks.

We must bear in mind that the achievements of the Greeks were always different from those of the Romans. While the Greeks made many beautiful things and had many excellent and revolutionary philosophers, doctors and scientists, they did not excel in the practical, day to day things that made life more comfortable and livable for the average citizen. For instance, when the Romans made Macedonia a province in 147 BC, the roads of Greece were notoriously poorly maintained, difficult to travel, and haunted by any number of thieves and murderers. One of the first things the Romans did after they had added Greek lands to their Empire was to build a broad road across the Macedonian penin- sula. Called the Egnatian way, this road connected the Adriatic and the Aegean seas. When Rome conquered Asian lands, the Egnatian way became an important path for Roman soldiers on their way east. The Romans built other roads throughout Grecian lands as well, making communications and trade much easier and safer for the Greek citizens of Rome.

Even the city of Athens owes something to Rome. In the second century AD, Athens was still a famous city, well known for its artistic treasures and monumental architecture, as well as for its university. While many tourists came to see the city's sights and many students came to learn from its brilliant professors, Athens was not prosperous, and its Golden Age was very much in the past. Many of the glories of Athens were falling into disrepair. Romans workers helped to preserve the city's famous buildings and temples, and Roman emperors contributed monuments of their own. Hadrian, who had a tremendous respect for Grecian culture and a deep love for Athens, built another Pantheon in the center of the city. The Athenians themselves erected an arch to honor Hadrian in 130 AD. On one side of the arch, which faces the old city, an inscription reads "This is Athens, the ancient city of Theseus." On the other side, a second inscription reads "This is the city of Hadrian and not of Theseus."

The Romans themselves, who were in awe of the Greeks' sophisticated intellectual and artistic accomplishments, were also aware that the two cultures had very different strengths and weaknesses. Virgil, whose epic poem *The Aeneid* describes the founding of Rome, includes a reference to the superiority of the Greeks in certain areas, and the superiority of the Romans in others. Speaking of the destiny of Rome, he says:

> Others will cast more tenderly in bronze
> their breathing figures, I can well believe,
> and bring more lifelike portraits out of marble;
> argue more eloquently, use the pointer
> to trace the paths of heaven accurately
> and accurately foretell the rising stars.
> Roman, remember by your strength to rule
> Earth's peoples - for your arts are to be these:
> to pacify, to impose the rule of law,
> to spare the conquered, battle down the proud.

The destiny of Rome was also, as we now know, to spread civilization throughout Europe, and to make it possible for people throughout the Empire to enjoy the cultural achievements, not just of the Romans, but of the Greeks and Egyptians as well.

Across the Aegean sea lay the province called Asia, which, along with seven other ancient provinces, makes up modern day Turkey. In Asia, we find Augustus Caesar's favorite city, Aphrodisias. Before Roman times, this city was a sacred site, dedicated to the goddess of love, Aphrodite. It remained an important religious and cultural center for many centuries and received countless pilgrims who journeyed to it from Asia and beyond.

[29]

After Augustus became Emperor, Aphrodisias gained favorite status in the eyes of the Rome. Her residents were exempted from paying taxes, perhaps because the people were so loyal to the Empire, or perhaps because Hadrian saw Aphrodisias as the real jewel in his crown. The city had a reputation for being hauntingly beautiful, not just because of its physical location, but because it possessed a seemingly inexhaustible supply of marble, which, creamy white in color and glittering with small crystals, was perhaps the finest in the world. Because of the abundance of this marble, Aphrodisian art flourished, and, for nearly six hundred years, Aphrodisian sculpture was unequaled in beauty and technique. Sculpture students flocked to Aphrodisias to learn from the masters, and Aphrodisian marble fetched the highest prices on the market. Many of the buildings of Aphrodisias were made of this luminescent marble as well, so that, one can well imagine, the city fairly gleamed.

To the north and east of the provinces that make up modern day Turkey lies Armenia, which was once a province of Rome. South of Armenia, the lands that are now Iran and Iraq were also once Roman, and, further back along the coast of the Mediterranean, the province called Syria still retains its ancient name.

In Syria, we find the third largest city of the Empire, Antiochia, which was one of the few cities of Rome with publicly lighted streets. In ancient times, Antiochia had a reputation for being wild and decadent. Disdainful Romans remarked that the lighted streets only permitted the Antiochians to carry their revelry all through the night. From Antiochia, we can follow a well-preserved Roman road inland, across the desert, where we come to Palmyra, which grew up in a fertile and prosperous oasis. Palmyra, which was well known in ancient times for its wealth, was built by the Romans, but, unlike most Roman cities, its building plan is not absolutely regular. The ruins of the city show that all of the streets do not meet at right angles, and the buildings are arranged in a asymmetrical fashion. This irregularity can be explained by the fact that before the Romans got to Palmyra, it was a well established Bedouin campsite. The Romans brought in their technology and created a city of stone and marble, following, to a certain extent, the haphazard arrangement of the more primitive encampments which had preceded them.

The Roman Empire extended along the coast of the Mediterranean, taking in modern day Lebanon, Israel and Jordan, as well as northern parts of Egypt. Here, as in Greece, the Romans confronted civilizations more ancient and advanced than their own. Jerusalem and Alexandria were both cosmopolitan cities with many beautiful buildings and temples and many learned and accomplished people. The city of Jerusalem, which had endured many wars and much hardship before the time of the Empire, was actually a thousand years older than the city of Rome. Alexandria, once capital of Egypt, was the second largest city in the Empire. Founded by the Greek Emperor, Alexander the Great, Alexandria was famous for its universities and for its libraries.

The most prominent feature of Alexandria, however, was its lighthouse, the first true lighthouse in history. Called the Pharos, this lighthouse was a 400 foot tower at whose top a wood fire was kept burning. The Pharos, which was built in 280 BC, was considered one of the Seven Wonders of the ancient world. Doubtless the Romans admired the great tower: they made smaller versions of it in port cities all over Italy. After the capture of Britain, they constructed the first northern lighthouses at Dover and Boulogne to help them cross the British Channel. The Dover lighthouse, partially crumbled, still stands. The Boulogne lighthouse was maintained and used until the middle of the seventeenth century.

Rome stretched on, into modern day Libya and Tunisia which made up the province of Africa. The city of Rome relied on African grain to feed its large population, and huge shipments of maize and wheat were sent across the Mediterranean in barges. Historically, governors of the African province made themselves quite wealthy overseeing the distribution of African foodstuffs, and the governorship of the province was a much sought after prize. The wealthy Roman leaders built many large and beautiful cities in Africa, such as Leptis Magna, Thugga and Timgad. These cities are now in ruins. Seen today, they can only give a hint of the opulence which they once possessed. Surrounded by arid land, the dusty remains of glorious theaters, public baths, temples and libraries testify to the splendor of the past.

The province to the west of Africa, called Mauretania, occupies the country we now know as Morocco. Like Africa, Mauretania was important because it provided fertile and sparsely populated land suitable for cultivation. The people of Mauretania were nomadic tribal herdsman who followed their sheep, goats and cattle from pasture to pasture. Most of these natives did not give up their ancient way of life to go and live in cities, and Roman rule was never fully accepted. Although the Mauri (as they were called by the Romans) did not completely fit into the Roman way of life, they did prove quite useful to the Roman army. Military leaders often employed Mauri in their light cavalry regiments, and one of the Emperor Trajan's best generals was a Mauri tribal chief.

From Mauretania, it is but a short boat ride across the straits of Gibralter and back onto the European continent to the lands we now know as Spain and Portugal, but which were then the three provinces Baetica, Lusitania and Tarraconensis. Spain (known to the Romans as Hispania) was the native land of two of the most important Emperors in the second century, Trajan and Hadrian. Both of these two men were born in a town called Italica in the province of Baetica. Although Italica was originally a small town, Hadrian, once he become Emperor, had it rebuilt in a magnificent style, constructing an amphitheater with enough seats for twenty five thousand spectators, and embellishing the city with many Greek-style sculptures. Although Italica became richer and bigger during Hadrian's rule, it may never have had a large enough population to justify the size of its amphitheater. The wealthier people of Italica did seem to live quite well and the ornate mosaics, which were once the floors of their elegant town houses, can be seen in an excavation of the old city.

North of Italica, lies Segovia, which, still an important city today, considers the huge, double arched Roman aqueduct which runs through its center one of its most prized and distinctive features. Known as El Puente, the aqueduct was built in the first century AD by the Emperors Trajan and Vespasian, and it carries water from the Río Frío into Segovia. The aqueduct is still in working order today, and even still supplied water to the higher parts of the city well into the twentieth century. Built entirely of perfectly fitted granite blocks, El Puente consists of one hundred and eighteen arches and stands ninety six feet high at its tallest point. The image of this structure can be found on coins minted in Segovia, and some residents of the city even have representations of it engraved upon their tombstones.

Although the Segovia aqueduct is impressive, it is overshadowed by the even larger, even longer aqueduct which stands just outside of Nîmes, France. Nîmes, which had access to the Mediterranean and lay on the major road between Italy and Spain, was one of the most important cities in all of ancient Gaul. If one can judge by the ruins which are still quite prominent in the city, Nîmes was clearly among the richest towns in the province. The town was built at the foot of a chain of barren hills. The tallest of these hills is still surmounted by a partially crumbled Roman tower which stands ninety two feet high and was once taller. The famous Pont du Gard aqueduct, which once carried water for thirty one miles, is tremendous proof of the skill and accuracy of Roman surveying and engineering. This aqueduct carried water so efficiently and so well that every day, thirty one million gallons of water used to travel from its source to the holding tanks which supplied the city. Over the course of this thirty one mile trip, the water only dropped a distance of fifty five feet.

Nîmes also contains what some regard to be the most perfectly preserved Roman temple in the world. The Maison Carrée, as it is known, has been the model for many government buildings, both ancient and modern, in America as well as in Europe. Modern day visitors to Washington DC might trace its outlines in the Supreme Court building. Not far from the Maison Carrée, the amphitheater of Nîmes is still used for bullfights. Although this amphitheater is much smaller than the Colosseum, only having a capacity for twenty four thousand spectators, it follows the same plan. Built of huge blocks of stone put together without mortar, the amphitheater seems to have escaped the ravages of time. Visitors to Nîmes can recreate the atmosphere of ancient Rome by watching a bullfight from the original Roman seats.

Gaul, much bigger than modern day France since it took in portions of Germany, Holland, Belgium and Switzerland, was one of the most heavily settled and most romanized of the provinces. In fact, sometimes the French proudly refer to their country as a second Italy. Many cities and towns throughout France were originally Roman, not the least of which is Paris, the most typically French city of all. Paris was actually a Gallic settlement before the Romans got to it, belonging to a tribe called the Parisii, who founded it during the third century BC. The Roman name for the city was Lutetia, which is believed to be a version of the Gallic name for the city. During the first century, Paris was completely rebuilt by the Romans. Although the city has been constantly growing and changing since that time, its Roman roots remain and can still be seen in several places. Ancient Roman baths lie beneath the Collège de France and beneath Rue Cluny in the Latin Quarter. A Roman theater has been excavated beneath the Lycée Saint Louis. While many of Paris's streets meander in serpentine paths, the straight and even boulevards, such as the Boulevard Saint Michel, are successors to the broad Roman roads which once lay there, connecting ancient Paris to the ancient world.

The Roman Empire extended its reach northward, beyond the European continent and into modern day England. Before the Romans got to England, the people who lived there were mostly Celtic tribes, who, unlike the Romans, did not have a highly complex or organized society. The Romans, whose civilization was eight hundred years old by the time they set foot on the island, introduced culture and technology to the native people. Many Roman towns of England have survived today to be important modern cities. London itself was created by the Romans: a Roman general named Aulus Plautius crossed the Thames River with his troops around 43 AD. At the point of his crossing, he had a bridge built and the town grew up around it. He chose the site for its strategic importance, called it Londinium, and it became the central point for all of the major roads in southern Britain. Just as all roads in Italy lead to Rome, all roads in Britain lead to Londinium. Little remains today of the ancient Roman city;we can still see fragments of the walls that once surrounded it, and the remains of a public bath have been discovered underground, but the plan of the city is not well known.

Other Roman cities in England have more obvious and tangible Roman roots, such as the resort town, Bath, which was known to the Romans as Aquae Sulis. Aquae Sulis had the only naturally occurring hot mineral springs in Britain. The Romans, who believed in the medicinal qualities of the waters, set up a town there, dedicated to the god Sul, a local deity whom they identified with their goddess, Minerva. By the end of the first century, they had built an extensive spa, with heated rooms, plunge baths, and circular baths. Two main pools were filled with hot water from the mineral springs, while the other baths, added on to the east and west ends, used other naturally occurring waters. Bath enjoyed almost four hundred years of popularity with the Romans and their successors, before the town was captured and sacked by the Angles and the Saxons from Germany.

Compared to the other provinces, England has relatively few large, monumental Roman structures which have survived into the present day. Roman-British civilization was, however, very real and very well developed. Probably the most enduring traces that the Romans left of themselves throughout Britain, Wales and Southern Scotland are the sometimes well-defined and sometimes ghostly outlines of their roads. Because Roman-British civilization was overtaken by barbarian tribes after the end of Roman rule, many of these roads fell into disuse and decay. The people of medieval Britain, ignorant of their Roman ancestors and awed by the straightness and solidity of the roads, sometimes believed they were built by giants longpast, or even by the Devil himself. Some of these "Devil's Causeways" as they were called, remained as the principle routes from one city to the next. Others virtually disappeared, leaving only their shadows in the straight lines of ever-present hedgerows.

The grandest Roman ruin in the United Kingdom is probably the great Hadrian's Wall, which extends seventy three miles across southern Scotland. Begun in 122 AD and completed in 128 AD, the wall served as a barrier and a stronghold for the Romans, who found the northern tribes of England more difficult to deal with than those in the south. The wall itself is fifteen feet high, and probably once had a six foot parapet on top of it. On either side of the wall, deep ditches were sunk into the ground as further protection against attack. All along the wall, which is built of stone and earth, the Romans made forts and watch towers from which they could survey the land to the south as well as to the north. For a time, Hadrian's Wall was effectively the border of the

Empire, although Roman influence extended northwards into Scotland, where another barrier, the Antonine Wall, further protected the Roman legions from attack.

And here, at the foggy Scottish frontier, we come to the end of Roman roads and the lands civilized by Roman laws and customs. Everywhere the Romans ruled, they left tangible evidence of their civilization and architectural skill. Although some of these traces of the Roman way of life are magnificent and striking, the true importance of Rome lies not in the physical structures it has left us, but in the more lasting impressions Roman language, law, customs and philosophy have made on our culture. Just as many modern cities were built on Roman foundations, so too many modern ideas, words, and ways of living grew out of ancient Roman culture. The Romans provided both the physical and the intellectual base from which society in Europe grew and developed. The vast size of the Roman Empire in 130 AD is more than matched by the deep and enduring importance of Roman civilization.

CHAPTER TWO:

A Roman Life

The founding fathers of America were lovers of ancient Italy. Not only did they model the principles of the new American Republic on those of the ancient Roman Republic, they also memorized speeches of great Roman orators, and some of them, such as Samuel Adams and Thomas Jefferson, even signed Latin names to their personal correspondence. American civilization was conceived by Italian scholars and fostered by Roman and Italian rules of justice, respect for property, and appreciation for personal freedom. When we say that our civilization descended from the Romans, we do not mean to imply that the Italians were the only contributors to our culture. Like ancient Rome, America is a gigantic melting pot, where people from all nations and all backgrounds contribute different ingredients to the brew of daily life. But our culture did come to us from a tradition which both consciously and unconsciously referred to ancient Italy.

Let us remember that "civilization" itself is a word with Roman roots. It found its way into the English language through Old French, and in turn, came into Old French from the original Latin. The roots of our civilization are likewise firmly grounded in ancient Italy, where many of our most basic beliefs and concepts first sprouted in the Mediterranean soil. The spread of Roman civilization during the time of the Empire came hand in hand with the growth of the Empire itself. During the last chapter we saw how the Romans constructed roads, cities, baths and other monuments wherever they ruled. These buildings are not simply an indication that the Romans existed throughout the vast area of their Empire, they are a proof that the Romans brought their life style to people of distant lands.

The Roman lifestyle included many things that we take for granted in modern times but which were by no means ordinary in the ancient world. Public buildings, such as courthouses and government offices, prove that the administration of the provinces was orderly, systematic and governed by law. Schools and libraries demonstrate that Romans valued knowledge and education. Public bath houses, which were much like today's health clubs, show that common people could find time for recreation. The Romans brought with them a higher standard of living, which, even if it could not be shared equally by everybody in their Empire, was far above the ordinary standards of the ancient world, where, in many places, the simple act of day to day survival was no mean feat. The stability and organization of the Roman way of life enabled people throughout the Empire to achieve higher levels of culture and productivity. The Romans did not simply conquer and subdue their neighbors: they civilized them.

One of the first reasons for Rome's success was military might. Roman armies, largely because of superior organization and their ability to adapt and adopt the weapons of people they had already conquered, won the vast majority of their battles, both on land and at sea. The Romans grew more and more successful as time went by because as their society grew, so did their armies. The Romans could often beat their adversaries simply because they had more fighting men in their regiments than did the enemy. Rome's early battles also prepared her for her later ones. By the time the Romans began to expand their Empire, they had become superb warriors because they learned the art of war from skillful enemies which they fought on the Italian peninsula.

Another reason for which the Romans were ultimately successful was that they did not give up easily. For instance, Julius Caesar was unable to capture Britain in 55 and 54 BC, when he made two separate forays across the English Channel. The tribes occupying Britain at the time did not have a highly organized society nor a well-equipped and efficient army, but they were fierce fighters. Relying on guerrilla warfare, which Julius's armies were not prepared to fight, they successfully defended their island from Caesar's forces. But Rome could not rest until the island formed a part of her Empire. Ninety years later, armies sent by the Emperor Claudius subdued the tribes, and Britannia became a Roman province. The Emperors of expanding Rome had a vision for her future; they saw Rome as the ruler of the western world, and they strove to fulfill her destiny.

When Claudius conquered Britain, his army included not simply Roman soldiers, but the most advanced weaponry of the day and even several elephants, which were transported across the Channel in huge barges. The elephants were used to drag heavy equipment through mud and up steep slopes. In addition to facilitating the Roman army's mobility, the elephants gave the Romans a significant psychological advantage over the British tribesmen who had never before seen such tremendously large and powerful animals. The Romans were probably introduced to the usefulness of elephants by their ancient enemies from Carthage, whose domesticated elephants were an important and highly visible element of their military success. In the third century BC., the famous Carthaginian military leader, Hannibal, brought no fewer than thirty-eight elephants with him in his valiant but ultimately doomed conquest of Rome. Hannibal and his army crossed the Alps in mid October of 218 BC, where ice and snow hampered their progress, and all but a few of the elephants foundered and perished of the cold. Some of the animals survived, however, and the image of an elephant soon appeared in Roman art and embossed on Roman coins: the elephant was adopted by Rome. Incidentally, the remains of a few of Hannibal's elephants, frozen over the centuries in the alpine snow, are even now being uncovered on the slopes north of Italy's Torino.

The highly advanced armies from Carthage also taught the Romans a thing or two about war at sea. Early in the third century BC, the Romans, who were in the process of taking over the entire Italian peninsula, came to the aid of a group of Italian mercenaries on the island of Sicily. Much of Sicily was ruled by Carthage, a city in modern day Tunisia. Carthage was rich, ancient, and a major sea power, while Rome was still an expanding, land-loving republic. While the Roman armies were fighting for their allies in Sicily, they began to think about driving the Carthaginians off of the island completely and annexing it to their kingdom. However, the Romans realized that in order to do this, they would have to defeat Carthage at sea. Undaunted by the fact that they had no experience on the water, Roman army engineers reportedly hauled a sunken Carthaginian ship off the floor of the sea and used it as a model for a fleet of Roman ships. Within a year, the Roman navy was equipped, and they set out to fight against the best fleet on the Mediterranean. Surprisingly, the Romans were victorious, and within the decade they had conquered not just the island of Sicily, but made themselves a sea power in the bargain.

Rome's armies were made up of professional soldiers in the pay of the state. During times of peace as well as during times of expansion, the soldiers of the army were employed building the roads, cities and monuments of the Empire. Rome's higher standard of living was therefore founded upon her military. Not only did the soldiers build many of the structures of the Empire, the money which successful campaigns brought into the state helped to finance their construction.

Although it is certainly true that some of the peoples conquered by the Roman army paid heavily for their resistance to Roman forces, most of the lands which became a part of Rome enjoyed more stability, prosperity and culture than their inhabitants could have dreamed of in pre-Roman times. This higher level of civilization was particularly noticeable in northern lands, which, before the Romans, were mostly dominated by relatively primitive tribes. In pre-Roman Britain, for example, tribesmen participated in magical religious rituals, including human sacrifice, and some of them were known to preserve the skulls of slain enemies and nail them to the porches of their houses. Some members of their society could read and write, but there was no school system, no organized government and no body of law.

Roman Britain, by contrast, was connected to the older civilizations of the Mediterranean. The Romans set up their colonies and cities, bringing with them schools for the children, works of literature and art from Rome and Greece, decorative and functional building methods, as well as such mundane, rudimentary things as spoons. Once the island was a part of the Empire, the people of Britain found themselves living in a more advanced, more organized, more comfortable society. Roman Britain, moreover, was in contact with the rest of the world. While in pre-Roman times a Celtic merchant might cross the Channel to trade with a native of the mainland, in Roman times, merchants suddenly had the opportunity to expand their trade into a real business. Although communication was slow, news from Rome travelled to Roman Britain, and news from Britain could travel back to Rome. The residents of Britannia were no longer a collection of people living in darkness; they were members of a more complex, more illuminated world.

The higher standard of living that the Romans brought to Britain was predicated upon something more important than manners and education; it was built upon a solid foundation of law and order, without which higher levels of culture would be impossible. The principles of Roman law were, and are, among the most valuable contributions the Roman people made to the world. The first formalization of Roman law took place around 450 BC, during the time of the Roman Republic. From its earliest days, Roman society was highly stratified; a vast gulf existed between the patrician upper and the plebeian lower classes. During the fifth century BC, the patrician class was in control of the legal as well as the political system of Rome. The plebeian class was not entirely without a voice in legal matters; they had special representatives, called tribunes, whose chief duty was make sure that patrician magistrates dealt fairly with plebeians. However, the plebeians believed they were at a disadvantage because the laws which governed the city were not written down. Because of this fact, they complained, patrician judges could unfairly manipulate laws so that it would seem that plebeians were always in the wrong when they came up against patricians in court. Chiefly because of the tribunes' complaints, the laws were drawn up and engraved upon twelve wooden tablets which were then set out in public, where anyone who was able could read them.

No record of the laws contained in the Twelve Tables has survived into the modern age, but during Cicero's time (106-43 BC), it was customary for school children to learn the text of the laws by heart. These laws, based upon custom and tradition, set out rules for the public behavior of citizens, gave instructions on the enactment of wills, and made pronouncements on property rights, family law, and the proper actions of the court. Although the laws were not very advanced from a legal point of view, their "publication" was tremendously important: it showed that Roman society was ready and willing to live by one formal, legal code, which would protect the rights of citizens from all walks of life. Roman society had embraced the principle of justice for all.

Over the course of Rome's history, the legal system grew and developed and the laws themselves changed, adapted and proliferated. In addition to the rules laid out by the Twelve Tables, jurists arguing cases could draw upon a large body of case law which were legal precedents describing past rulings of magistrates and opinions of jurists. Over time, various textbooks of law appeared, along with law schools, and the special new profession of lawyers. Around 527 AD, Justinian, who was the Emperor of the Eastern Roman Empire, ordered all of the law books, precedents and formal written laws reviewed and revised. He then had these laws published in standardized form known as the *corpus iuris civilis*, or the Body of Common Law. The Justinian Code, as it came to be known, formed the basis for the legal system in most modern western nations. The Napoleonic Code, which governs the legal system in France, was directly modelled upon it, as are many modern laws in Germany. America's state of Louisiana, which was a once a French territory, still uses many laws from the Napoleonic Code. The English developed a system of their own, called common law, which, although it was not directly based upon Roman law, was influenced by it. The Roman basis of modern American, English and European law is readily apparent in legal language: legal terms, to this day, are Latin phrases.

Roman legal philosophers, like America's founding fathers, had a high regard for the forces of justice and fairness, as well as for the rights of individuals in a society. Many of the concepts embodied in the American Constitution come directly or indirectly out of ancient Italian legal thought. Like our American forefathers, the Romans believed that no man could be punished for what he thought. They also believed that no man could be made to defend a cause against his will. They believed that justice was an

Mosaic of Emperor Justinian, author of the Justinian Code

Mosaics from the Bath of Marciana, Ostia Antica

Street scene at Pompei

impersonal force, independent of the foibles of human beings, and that the spirit, rather than the letter of the law was its essence. Like many later philosophers, they believed in a natural law which superseded laws made by human beings, and because of this, their laws were always open to change. If a particular rule could be demonstrated to be unfair, it could be modified to correspond more closely to ideal justice.

One of the greatest of Roman legal writers was Marcus Tullius Cicero, who was born in Arpino, outside of Rome, in 106 BC. Cicero was a highly educated orator who used his eloquence both to further his own political career and to argue cases in court. He is most famous for exposing the plots of Catiline, a military leader who planned to overthrow the Roman government. Because of Cicero's impassioned speeches, Catiline was eventually executed. As a lawyer, Cicero also successfully defended many people who were accused of crimes against the state, and he was well known for his ability to move the jury to anger or pity as well as to reduce them to laughter. Cicero's philosophy was based upon a respect for reason, education, and culture, and an abhorrence of violence and extremism. In addition to being a jurist, he was a tremendously prolific writer who composed hundreds of letters and essays on topics ranging from ethics and political theory to his own feelings about growing old.

Throughout the ages, many western scholars have considered Cicero to be one of the finest writers and thinkers in history. Rhetoricians regarded him as a "model orator who is a model of moral excellence." Whole schools of rhetoric have grown up around Cicero's recorded speeches: some teachers in the Middle Ages would reject their students' work if it was not written in Cicero's style. The famous Renaissance humanist, Cardinal Bembo, modelled his own writing so closely after Cicero's, his every phrase echoed the structure of a phrase of Cicero's. Cicero was not tremendously important as a philosophical thinker, but his philosophical writings transmitted many Greek ideas into Roman thought and consequently, into the Latin language. By importing Greek phrases into Latin, Cicero gave Rome its philosophical vocabulary. Because of Cicero's writing, we have such words as quality, individual, moral, element, difference and infinity.

[43]

Voltaire, the great French writer of the eighteenth century, said "We honor Cicero, who taught us how to think." Cicero's contemporary, Julius Caesar, who was a brilliant writer as well as an esteemed military leader, also paid tribute to Cicero, saying "It is better to have extended the frontiers of the mind than to have pushed back the boundaries of the Empire."

Modern readers of Cicero's speeches are struck not only by the ideas that they express, but also by their extraordinarily fine style. During Cicero's time, educated people paid a great deal of attention to the way they expressed their thoughts, choosing words not simply for their meanings, but also for their sounds and rhythms. Even works of Latin prose are as carefully written as poetry: the Romans enjoyed and appreciated their language, and being able to use it well was a mark of good breeding. In fact, one of the primary focusses of a Roman education was upon spoken and written eloquence.

In the early days of the Roman Republic, education was largely a private matter. It was up to the family to teach its children social arts and proper Roman values. Around 250 BC, Greek-influenced schools began to spring up in Roman lands, and, eventually, public education became available. Until the age of twelve, Roman boys and girls went to school together, where they learned to read and write and studied mythology. After the age of twelve, it was usually only the upper class boys who continued their education. They learned to read in Greek, and memorized Latin speeches, practicing to be eloquent and skillful orators themselves. People who were good speakers, like Cicero, were well positioned for careers in public service, and had the chance to attain a considerable amount of power and prestige.

The Greek influence in the realm of Roman education was particularly strong. In the last chapter we pointed out that the Greeks' major contribution to the ancient world was an intellectual one. The Romans recognized the excellence of Greek masters in the areas of philosophy and medicine, and were eager to absorb Greek knowledge and ideas into Roman culture. Accordingly, many Greeks came to Rome as tutors for wealthy Roman children, and many Greek poems and plays were translated into Latin. In fact, if the Romans had not welcomed Greek culture into their society, many works of Greek art and literature would not have survived to the modern day. In addition to having a Greek tutor in Rome, a well bred Roman might further his studies at a Greek university. Cicero, for example, when he wanted to improve his oratorical style, left Rome to study at the Academy in Athens. After spending six months in Athens, he went on to Asia Minor, where he sought the instruction of Julius Caesar's Greek tutor.

The most highly educated Romans were proud of their ability to read and speak Greek, much as well educated Americans are proud of a facility in French. Although the Romans certainly appreciated Greek intellectual contributions, they tended to look down on the Greeks themselves,whom they regarded as effeminate and duplicitous. When Cicero returned from his sojourn in Greek speaking lands and went back into Roman legal practice, he found himself quite un-popular with the Roman crowd. He was nick-named "Egghead" and "the Greek": nobody intended either term to be a compliment. A large number of Greeks immigrated to Rome during the first century BC when Greece was invaded by Persian armies. Many of these Greeks were highly skilled doctors, scientists, artists and teachers, while others were equally skilled swindlers, quacks and social climbers. Even after a lifetime in Rome, many Greeks did not bother to learn to speak Latin, a fact which irked some Romans. The satirist Juvenal did not have a particularly high regard for the average Greek in Rome. He wrote:

> What do you take
> That fellow's profession to be? He has brought a whole bundle
> Of personalities with him - schoolmaster, rhetorician,
> Surveyor, artist, masseur, diviner, tightrope-walker,
> Magician or quack, your versatile hungry Greekling
> Is all by turns. Tell him to fly - he's airborne.

In addition to their contributions in philosophy, art and literature, the Greeks also provided the Romans with the most advanced medicines and medical techniques of the day, which, characteristically, the Romans were able to organize into functioning medical systems. The Romans created the first hospitals in the western world, as well as the first formal schools of medicine.

[45]

They were also the first society to set up organized military medical services which were paid for by government taxes. The two greatest doctors of antiquity, however, were both Greeks. The first, Hippocrates, who is often considered the father of medicine, practiced and taught surgery on the Greek island of Cos during the fifth century BC. The second great doctor of antiquity was Galen, a Roman citizen born of Greek parents in modern day Turkey during the second century AD. Galen moved to Rome, under the auspices of the Emperor Marcus Aurelius, where in addition to serving as the Emperor's personal physician, he taught classes and gave demonstrations of dissection and surgery. Many of Galen's treatises and theories survived unchallenged into the sixteenth century. Because the Romans imported many of their doctors and teachers of medicine from Greece, Greek, rather than Latin, became the language of medical science. To this day, medical terms are often Greek phrases.

Although travel was difficult during the time of the Empire, safe road systems and sea-worthy ships meant that people could do such modern-sounding things as study abroad for a year, or take a sightseeing tour of historic foreign cities. In fact, in some ways travel for the Roman citizen was easier than it is today: not only were there no borders to cross, and thus no need for visas or passports, but the currency was the same everywhere, and throughout at least the Western half of the realm, the official language was Latin. In the East, although Latin was understood by most educated people, Greek remained the official language. Because it was possible to travel over the vast distances of the Empire, the city of Rome found itself at the center of a bustling commercial and cultural world. Greeks were not the only people who came to enjoy the prosperity of the capital. People from as far away as Asia and Britain came to live in Rome, bringing with them different customs and traditions as well as foreign goods and exotic foodstuffs.

Not only did people go to live in Rome from all corners of the Empire, the Romans themselves, when they could get time off from their work and responsibilities, might set off to see the sights of the Empire: the upper class Roman was the prototype of the modern tourist. Although travelling was definitely a costly and a time consuming affair, many residents of Rome, after reading their guidebooks and histories, would set out across the Mediterranean to see the famous sights of Greece, Asia Minor, and Egypt, bringing back souvenirs and a better understanding of the world. By the second century AD, tourism had become a real industry in the Empire, and there are even reports of famous places being ruined by the volume of foreigners and souvenir seekers who flocked to them. The town of Delphi in Greece, which in Roman times was renowned for its artistic treasures, became a real tourist trap, which was reportedly so mobbed with guides a traveller could not have moment to himself. Fewer tourists made it as far as Egypt, but those who did could not resist scratching graffiti into the bases of the Great Pyramids. Tourists might return to Rome bearing terra cotta replicas of famous statues, or little flasks of water from the Nile. The relative ease of travelling meant that the Empire was a well mixed and highly cosmopolitan place.

Another reason for the cosmopolitan nature of the Empire was the enforced resettling of various populations from far away provinces. Sometimes, groups of people were simply sent to live in sparsely populated areas to relieve over-crowding in their native lands. Inhabitants of the city of Palmyra, for instance, were dispatched to guard Hadrian's Wall in northern Britain. Nîmes, in France, had a large population of Egyptians, resettled from Alexandria. The Roman system of slavery was also responsible for a great deal of cultural intermixing throughout the Empire. While the Empire was still expanding, Roman armies would sometimes capture entire cities and send their inhabitants into slavery in other lands where they would eventually become a part of the permanent population.

The Roman slave system, an integral part of its culture, was not exactly the same as slave systems in more recent cultures. Slaves were people from all walks of life, with all differentprofessions and levels of education. Some slaves were employed as heavy laborers, building roads, bridges and monuments. Others were put to work as painters, musicians, teachers, and even doctors. Roman slaves were generally humanely treated, probably because even in their inferior status, they were always recognized as people. Slaves were protected by the law, and a slave could bring a civil suit against his master if he was mistreated. In the early days of the Republic, even Roman citizens could sell themselves into slavery if they became heavily in debt. The Roman practice of freeing slaves was also quite common, and the children of freedmen could become full-fledged Roman citizens. Many patrician masters left instructions in their wills providing for the freeing of all their slaves upon their deaths. Although some slaves certainly had hard lives with little chance for advancement, many lived to see their children and grandchildren become well respected and powerful citizens.

Although our own modern life is obviously far removed from that of the Roman Empire, many of the every day concerns of the Romans were similar to our own. Inhabitants of big cities were concerned about high crime rates, violence and juvenile delinquency. Even well-born youths were known to overindulge in drink and wander through the streets at night, picking fights and causing trouble. Nowadays, we are shocked to hear that the chil dren of prominent politicians, actors and public personalities are caught driving drunk, selling drugs or participating in bar room brawls. Back in the days of the Romans, the sons of prominent people were known to be drunk and disorderly. Many patrician teenagers joined street gangs which robbed and mugged innocent passersby, while others engaged in acts of vandalism. It was even common knowledge that the young Emperor Nero used to go out marauding at night, robbing and harassing people he found in the streets. Ancient Rome also suffered from certain problems which have been remedied in modern times. One of the major disadvantages of the ancient city was a lack of street lights. After dark, the shadowy streets became a virtual jungle. Bands of disorderly youths could count on the darkness to shield their identities, so that even the most well born young man was not afraid of having his misbehavior discovered and punished. The streets of Rome were also not well marked. Unlike the orderly cities in the Empire, Rome was not a planned city and its narrow streets were not laid out in a grid pattern. In the dark, even a lifelong resident of the city might have difficulty finding his way home, especially if he had been drinking. Because of these problems, well-bred Romans tended to stay inside after nightfall, not daring to risk a stroll through the dangerous night life of the city.

Other problems that ancient Rome shared with modern cities were noise and overcrowding. Like many modern cities, ancient Rome did not have space to comfortably house all of its inhabitants. The wealthiest Romans lived in private houses, but most people in the center of the city lived in apartment buildings which were known as insulae. As the population continued to expand, the insulae were built higher and higher. Over time, various laws were enacted, designed to limit the height of the insulae, which were often cheaply constructed and dangerous. Those insulae which were built to house the city's poor were like modern day tenements: they were infested with rats and their roofs were prone to collapsing. They were also known to be highly flammable fire traps.

The problem of noise in ancient Rome is also well documented. Because there was so much pedestrian traffic down the narrow streets during daylight hours, horse drawn carts and chariots were outlawed from sunrise to sunset. During the night, when the streets were empty, the chariot traffic moved in, bringing deliveries to stores and businesses, and transporting building materials to works in progress. Although this arrangement cut down on street congestion during the day, it also ensured that nights would be filled with the sounds of carts and horses. Juvenal, a writer of the first century, complained that the noise from the street outside of his apartment was so great he could not sleep. "Insomnia causes more deaths among Roman invalids/ Than any other factor," he claimed.

Since living comfortably within the city was difficult, many wealthy Romans maintained villas outside of Rome, to which they could retreat for some peace and quiet, especially during the hot summer months. For the wealthier Roman, the home was a place of refuge. Roman houses were constructed with a high wall facing the street, to shut out unwanted sights, sounds and smells. The house was built around a sheltered courtyard which provided a pleasant and quiet prospect for its inhabitants. These courtyards were adorned with statues, plants, and marble columns. Many homes had elaborately painted walls, depicting characters from mythology as well as more mundane scenes and geometric patterns. Some were decorated with false windows, showing agreeable landscapes and good weather outside, while the floors were often lined with mosaic tiles.

The main room of the house was the atrium, which served as a reception room for the family and visitors. The atrium also contained portraits of the family and an altar to the family gods, known as Lares. Roman bedrooms were generally small, rectangular rooms, reserved for sleeping, and many houses had separate bedrooms for summer and winter use. There were likewise summer and winter dining rooms, as well as parlors, rooms to hold the family archives, picture galleries, terraces, and in some houses, bathrooms. In addition, of course, were the slave quarters, storage rooms and kitchens. Country houses and expensive villas followed the same general plan as city houses, but on a much grander scale, incorporating more space and allowing for inviting views of the countryside. The Roman home, whether a modest dwelling in the city or an expensive country retreat, demonstrated the Roman desire to live comfortably and well.

It has often been said that unlike the Greeks, the Romans designed their buildings to be enjoyed from the inside, rather than from the outside. This type of design reflects not simply the Roman's taste for comfort, but also their belief in the importance of the family. The idea of the family as a self-contained unit began in the early days of Rome. Originally, the father of the family, or pater familias had absolute authority over all of the people in his household. He was even given the power of life and death over his children; Roman law authorized him to carry out capital punishment if his son or daughter committed a grievous crime. He was likewise able to repudiate his wife, throwing her out into the street with no money or possessions, if, for any reason, he grew tired of her. As time went by, the power of the pater familias declined, but the idea of the family as the basic unit of society persisted into the modern day.

By the second century AD, the pater familias, although still recognized as the head of the family, had become more or less the equal of his wife, at least in family matters. Legally, there were several different ways that a couple could be married. The oldest form of marriage, *cum mano,* made the wife the virtual slave of her husband, depriving her of her possessions and of her freedom. By the second century, however, cum mano marriages were rare. Other forms of marriage were more equal; in *sine mano* marriages, which became the commonest form of union during the first and second centuries, the wife retained her personal property along with the right to initiate divorce proceedings against her husband. Marriage was an important institution then as it is now, and some ancient Roman wedding customs are still in use today. The tradition of placing a simple wedding band on the second to last finger of the left hand, for instance, comes out of the Roman betrothal ceremony. The Romans believed that a nerve in this finger was directly connected to the heart, and that placing a ring upon it would ensure marital felicity.

Of course, then, as now, no ring could guarantee the compatibility or happiness of a married couple, and divorce was almost as venerable a Roman custom as marriage. By the second century AD, divorce was just as common in Rome as it is today in America - if not more so. Roman divorce law was quite liberal, allowing a woman to take back her dowry at the dissolution of the marriage, and allowing both parties to remarry as frequently as they wished. And, if we are to believe the satirists of the time, it often happened that Romans wished to remarry quite frequently indeed. Although in the early part of the era, divorce was looked down upon by society and nobody would think of divorcing unless his or her spouse had committed some terrible sin, eventually divorce became accepted as quite ordinary. It was even fairly common for divorced people to remarry each other eventually after a series of other marriages. Not only did people get divorced because they no longer cared for one another, they also might divorce in order to remarry somebody who had more money than their current spouse. Cicero, at the age of sixty, for instance, divorced his wife of thirty three years, the mother of his children, in order to marry a wealthy girl of fifteen.

The liberalized divorce laws, along with the increasing freedom of well-born women to do as they pleased, inspired some writers of the first two centuries to lament that women were acting "too much like men." Juvenal, in his Satires, complained about women discussing politics in the forum, and derided women who worked with weights and competed with men in athletic competitions. In fact, some of these writings of the first century AD sound very much like those written in America during the twentieth century. Moralists of the day were concerned that women were not as interested as they should have been in having children and obeying their husbands. The complaints of these writers draw attention to the fact that, even though women were not afforded the same legal protection or political rights as their brothers, their position in society was no longer one of subservience, and was beginning to approach equality. The freedom of women to go about on their own and to hold personal property is in sharp contrast to the restrictions which the ancient Greeks imposed upon women, who were always regarded as inferior to men in every way and were never granted the highly touted rights of the Greek citizen.

Roman cities provided their inhabitants with several advantages, among them free or inexpensive admission to the public baths. A public bath house in a Roman city was often far more than a place to go and bathe; it was a social and cultural center. The huge complexes which housed some of the larger baths, such as those built by the Emperor Caracalla in Rome could accommodate thousands of bathers. They also frequently had libraries, as well as places to exercise, steam rooms and saunas, and employed professional trainers and masseurs. Both men and women frequented the baths, although they bathed separately, and people from all levels of society found time to visit them, sometimes as often as every day. In fact, Roman bath houses served very much the same function as health clubs do today in America. Paintings and mosaics depicting bikini-clad young women lifting small weights in a Roman bath could easily be mistaken for a modern representations of college students engaged in an aerobics class.

In addition to going to the bath houses, the people of Roman towns enjoyed spectacles, ranging from productions of plays in open air theaters, to chariot races, to gladiatorial contests. Gladiatorial contests have received a great deal of attention and have often been pointed to as evidence that, for all of their organizational and architectural skill, the Romans were blood-thirsty barbarians at heart. Gladiatorial "games" came in many forms, most of them ending in death for one or more of the participants. In essence, a gladiatorial show consisted of a fight, either between two or more men, or between men and various animals. Sometimes the men would be armed, giving them an advantage over animals or other men; sometimes they would be unarmed and at the mercy of the wild beasts or armed fighters pitted against them. Thousands of wild animals captured in Africa might be killed in a single day's spectacle at the Colosseum in Rome. Sometimes, of course, the beasts would win, and the men sent to fight them would die. Gladiators themselves were usually convicted criminals who had been sentenced to death and then sent through rigorous training schools. Although gladiators were expected to fight to the death and thus fulfill their sentences, a really superb fighter might eventually win his freedom.

Although these blood-thirsty and murderous shows might sound foreign and repulsive to us, we should bear in mind that the public taste for this kind of spectacle has not been extinguished. Spanish bullfights, in which people applaud the matador as he pierces the heart of a tortured and enraged bull are still very popular. Although we do not expect our American prize-fighters to punch each other until they actually die, we do cheer them on until one has knocked the other into a bloody stupor. Finally, if we think of the gladiatorial shows as a prolonged and dramatic execution of convicted criminals, we must remember that many people in this country not only favor the death penalty, but think that executions ought to be public.

Although gladiatorial shows were certainly very popular entertainment in the cities of Rome, other, less violent, but equally extravagant exhibitions were also put on for the public to enjoy during the many Roman holidays. Trained performing animals such as we might expect to see in a modern day circus were quite common, as were acrobats and jugglers. Horse and chariot races were run in Rome's Circus Maximus, and the public used to bet on the outcome. Sometimes whole city squares were flooded and mock naval battles were staged for an enthusiastic audience. All of these shows entailed a great deal of expense, but most were free to the public. The cost was frequently borne by the government, but was also sometimes taken on by a highly placed and wealthy public official.

Cynical people might say that the shows were put on for one reason only; to distract the poor and the jobless from their misery and thereby keep them from rebelling against the state. However, the practice of donating money to provide entertainment for the public was not just a convenient way to placate a potentially restless mob. It can also be seen as a sign of genuine interest in giving something back to society. From the very early days of Rome, the wealthiest citizens gave money to benefit people who were less fortunate than they. Some of the wealthy put on shows, while others built schools, baths, or public parks. When Cicero was a public official in Sicily, instead of putting on shows, he assisted debtors, provided money for dowries and ransom for victims of piracy. Philanthropy was a well used Roman institution, which underscores the advanced nature of Italian culture. For centuries, Italian citizens have understood and embraced their debt to the society which created them.

Although many of our modern customs grew out of Roman customs, the single major way in which our lives have been influenced by the Romans of two thousand years ago is probably through words. That nearly fifty percent of our English vocabulary comes from Latin is only a small part of the story. More important is the fact that the great Roman writers of the Republican and early Imperial age are still widely read and studied in our schools, American, English and European alike. Most of us probably do not remember a great deal about these famous Latin writers, but some of their words and sayings are so much a part of our everyday perceptions that we are shocked to hear that they were first spoken in Latin so many centuries ago. A famous quotation from Cicero inspired a well known American song: "There is no place more delightful than home." Virgil tells us that "Love conquers all," and Seneca noted that "It is not quantity but quality which matters." Other familiar sayings such as "Better late than never," "No one knows until he tries," "Let the buyer beware," "To err is human" and "There is no accounting for tastes," were all familiar Latin proverbs. Perhaps we have not all read the works of Cicero, nor studied Horace, nor committed Ovid to memory, but none of us can escape the influence of Roman philosophy and Roman writing. Even the sign we might hang outside our front gate reading "Beware of the dog" had a Roman precursor: a similar sign, showing a dog and words "Cave Canem," ("Beware of the dog") was a fairly common sight on the floors of Roman homes.

It would certainly be an exaggeration to say that the people who lived during the time of the Roman Empire were people just like us who saw life in the same way as we do today. There are obviously huge differences, not just because of the tremendous technological gulf which separates our lives from theirs, but because of religious, social and historical matters as well. However, the people of the Roman Empire were, without any doubt, our forefathers in terms of the language we speak, the laws that we live by, and the ideals that we cherish. While many of the people of Europe seem to recognize and appreciate their Roman backgrounds, the people of America rarely do. Perhaps the reason that the people of Europe and England embrace their Italian heritage so eagerly is because the ancient ruins which populate their lands constantly remind them of their Roman roots.

In America we have no Roman ruins to jog our memories, but our culture nonetheless grows out of Italian soil. America's forefathers, like the early Romans themselves, did not hesitate to incorporate elements of other civilizations into their own. Because they admired the Romans, they consciously sought to emulate the Roman Republic when they fashioned the government of the United States. But the Italian influence in America is far more than the result of an artificial seeding of Roman ideas in the Constitution. Roman ideas and ideals have been a part of Western consciousness for almost two thousand years; they have grown so much a part of our lives, that we could not separate them out if we tried. Our civilization, like the word civilization itself, has Italian roots.

Arte Etrusca, the Mater Matuta from the *Museo Archeologico* in Florence

CHAPTER THREE

The Roots Of Rome

Rome, as we are told in the proverb, was not built in a day. The vast and complex Empire was laboriously established over hundreds of years of war, expansion, and, finally, peace. The city which would create the Empire grew from humble beginnings as one of many small towns in central Italy. Originally just an ordinary village, Rome grew to be the military and cultural leader of all of the other villages around it. Meanwhile, the social and political structure of the city became increasingly sophisticated, and Rome emerged as a Republic, administered by a body of elected officials. As Rome's power expanded, her government changed. By the beginning of the Christian era, Rome was ruled by an Emperor, and the Western world was ruled by Rome.

How and why did the Romans become such a dominant people? Ancient historians (particularly Roman ancient historians) say that Rome's greatness was decreed by the gods. Later historians, writing from a Christian perspective, would, interestingly enough, say basically the same thing: the Roman Empire was created for the specific purpose of spreading the word of Christ. Putting aside for the moment these theories of divine assistance, there are many reasons for the phenomenal success of the Romans. In their earliest days, the excellent location of their city contributed to their growth and prosperity. More important for Rome's triumph, however, was the Roman people's organizational ability, coupled with an openness to outside influences, and a belief in their destiny as rulers of the world.

[57]

The early history of Rome is shrouded by folkloric and magical beliefs. For thousands of years, historians, poets and myth-makers have creatively described the foundation of the city, and many legends have grown up around Rome's background. The most popular legend involves twin brothers named Romulus and Remus. According to the legend, Romulus and Remus were the sons of a woman named Rhea Silvia, a Vestal Virgin who was raped by Mars, the god of war. When the infant twins were newly born, they were abandoned to die by the banks of the Tiber river. The babies did not perish, however, because they were discovered and suckled by a female wolf, and then adopted by a shepherd and his wife. Romulus and Remus grew up to plan and lay the foundations for a new city in a solemn religious ceremony which allegedly took place in the year 753 BC. During an argument soon afterwards, Romulus killed Remus, and the city was thereafter named "Rome" for the surviving brother. Romulus became the first Roman king. After his death, some legends say that his father, Mars, carried him up into the heavens where, in later years, he was worshipped as the Roman god Quirinus.

Another familiar legend formed the basis for the epic poem, *The Aeneid*, which was composed in the first century BC by the great Latin writer Virgil. According to Virgil's story, the twins Romulus and Remus were the direct descendants of a Trojan warrior named Aeneas. After the Greeks destroyed Troy in 1184 BC, Aeneas supposedly fled with his family, looking for a site on which to establish a new major city. After long travels, he landed in Italy, where he married the daughter of a king and founded the Roman race. Several generations later, Rhea Silvia was born into the family, and she eventually gave birth to Romulus and Remus.

Of course, the stories of Aeneas, Romulus and Remus are legends rather than history, and do not really tell us a great deal about the actual events in Italy before the emergence of Rome. However, just because these legends contain fanciful elements does not mean that all of the information they convey is unreliable. Many recent historians, for instance, agree that the first king of infant Rome probably was a man named Romulus. Although the divine descent (and ascent) of this first king is from the mythological realm, Rome probably was founded in or around the year 753 BC. While in the past, historians have argued that the city emerged slowly out of the hills, more recent evidence indicates that Rome was indeed founded by a religious rite, and its establishment was indeed a specific historical act. The mythological elements of the story are also important for what they tell us about the Romans' perception of themselves and of their history. The earliest Romans felt themselves to be descended from the gods, and they believed that a divine power was ultimately behind the creation and development of their city. This belief in itself meant that Rome was qualitatively different from earlier village settlements: the Romans felt they had to live up to the expectations of the gods.

The story of Aeneas is equally important to our understanding of ancient Rome. Unlike Romulus, Aeneas was not, as far as we know, an historical person. While it is undoubtedly true that many foreigners came to the Italian peninsula during the second millennia BC, there is no reason to believe that the ancient Romans were descended from foreign warriors. The story of Aeneas does show us that the Romans of the first century (when the poem was written) wanted to believe in themselves not simply as the rulers of the world, but also as the legitimate inheritors of the earlier, advanced cultures of the Mediterranean. *The Aeneid* tries to fit Rome's story into the stories of ancient Greece. Virgil's poem is basically a continuation of Homer's famous Greek epics the *Iliad* and the *Odyssey*. Believers in the story of Aeneas can therefore see the *Iliad* and the *Odyssey* as a part of their own culture. The Romans were greedy in a sense: not satisfied with their own literature, they took Greek literature and made it their own.

Rome's ability to adopt the stories, beliefs and talents of foreign cultures was an important part of her success. In the eighth century BC, when Rome was founded, Italy was populated by a wide variety of different people. The Romans were just one of several Latin speaking tribes which inhabited the Latin plain. Other, non-Latin tribes shared the peninsula, along with Greek and Phoenician colonists. Although the Romans were frequently at war with these other societies, one of the reasons that Rome rose to prominence was because the Romans accepted and learned from many outside influences. The Romans came into contact with other civilizations through trade as well as through war, and Rome welcomed foreign talents as well as foreign goods.

As we have already pointed out, Grecian civilization contributed a great deal to Roman culture. At the time of Rome's foundation, Greek cities dotted the southern coast of the Italian peninsula, and even after Rome became an Empire, some of these cities retained their Greek names along with distinctly Greek atmospheres. Naples, for instance, was originally a Greek colony: its ancient name, Neapolis, meant "new city" in Greek, and Greek was still the first language of many Neapolitan during the days of the Empire. In Rome's early days, Greek art, literature, philosophy, science and government exerted an undeniable influence upon the younger, relatively unsophisticated Roman people. And yet, not to downplay the contributions of Greece, the profoundest and longest lasting impressions on Roman culture were not made by Grecian colonists. From the middle of the eight century BC until the middle of the third century BC, the strongest, most advanced and most important people on the Italian Peninsula were not the Romans nor the Greeks, but rather the Etruscans.

Who were the Etruscans, where did they come from and what were they like? These are questions that have intrigued historians and archaeologists for centuries. The Etruscans are almost always referred to as a "mysterious" people, or an "enigmatic" people, or a "perplexing" people: one runs out of adjectives. Like many other ancient groups, the Etruscans have disappeared, taking with them their language, their literature and their history. Although our understanding of this "lost" people is advancing practically every day, we still do not know a great deal about them. While many Etruscan inscriptions have been translated, Etruscan literature did not survive the ages, and Etruscan history has only come down to us in unsatisfactory ways: told, for example, by patriotic Greeks and Romans who did not like them, or who wanted to identify them with characters from mythology. We do have some beautiful examples of their art, however, most of it gleaned from their elaborate tombs, and we do also know that they, more than any other foreign group, provided the Romans with the tools which would lead them to glory.

The Etruscans lived in central and northern Italy, in the region that is now called Tuscany. According to ancient tradition, there were twelve Etruscan cities. Each of these cities was politically independent, but they formed a loose confederation, probably centered around religious festivals. Although none of the cities was actually on the sea, the Etruscans were an important sea power. Because of this, they were in contact with all of the various civilizations of the Mediterranean, as well as with the other cultures of the Italian peninsula. They traded with the Greeks, the Phoenicians, the Assyrians, the Carthaginians and the Egyptians. Like the ancient Romans, the Etruscans owed a measure of their success to the richness of the Italian peninsula. Because Etruria had abundant supplies of metal, the Etruscans were among the wealthiest people in the Mediterranean. Ancient descriptions tell us that they lived luxuriously: even their slaves were well dressed. Their capabilities at sea also added to their wealth: Greek writers, possibly jealous of their maritime dominion, described them as fearful pirates.

Etruscan cities dominated northern Italy while Etruscan ships commanded the Mediterranean. For over a century, Etruscans also ruled Rome itself. The extent of Etruria's control over Rome is open to debate. While some scholars believe that the Etruscans actually captured the city and ruled it as a vassal state, others think that Etruscans were simply accepted into Roman society. Most scholars agree, however, that from 625 BC until 510 BC, Rome had Etruscan kings. Under the administration of these kings, Rome became a true urban community. Etruscans were masters of irrigation, drainage and canal digging. Contemporary Etruscan cities were more advanced than fledgling Rome: they had sewers and proper drainage, solid rock roads, temples and bridges. During the years that Etruscans ruled Rome, they transformed it with their skills in architecture, engineering and city planning.

The Etruscans are responsible, in fact, for many of the most distinctive characteristics of the city of Rome. They drained and cleared the area that was to become the Roman Forum, which was formerly a marshy, low-lying area, used sporadically as a cemetery, and turned it into the economic and political heart of the city. Etruscan engineers laid the foundation for Rome's sewers. They dug subterranean drainage channels, which the Romans called *cuniculi,* that funnelled surface water from places where it was not needed out into the fields. Hitherto uncultivated areas were converted into productive cropland. The Etruscans built the main sewer of Rome, the *Cloaca Maxima,* as well as the Circus Maximus, and some of ancient Rome's major temples. The Romans owe the Captoline hill, the seat of their government, to the establishment of an Etruscan temple there.

According to ancient tradition, the Etruscans taught the Romans not only how to dig sewers, but also how to build roads, bridges, tombs, temples and houses. The Roman art of town planning was reportedly learned from the Etruscans, and the Roman house, as well as the Roman temple, was built on an Etruscan plan. The Etruscans brought the alphabet to the Romans and taught them how to write. Etruscan gods and Etruscan mythology became integrated into Roman religion. Romans borrowed Etruscan ceremonies, such as the triumph: a victory parade in which generals displayed their soldiers, booty and prisoners of war to the civilian population. Romans appropriated Etruscan symbols of power, such as the magistrate's chair and the fasces, a bundle of rods tied around an axe which symbolized the king. The fasces, a familiar symbol to the Romans, also became a familiar symbol in the twentieth century when Mussolini took it as the emblem of his party: the word fascism is derived from Mussolini's adoption of the Etruscan image. Although it is impossible to say exactly how much Roman culture ultimately came from Etruscan sources, it is quite clear that the Etruscans were a major influence on the development of Rome.

The influence of ancient Etruria was not confined to Roman civilization. When the Etruscan era was at its height during the sixth century BC, Etruscan merchants and warriors travelled far and wide. The Etruscans ranged over the entire Mediterranean in their ships, and Etruscan artifacts have been found in every major port of Greece, as well as in Egypt, Tunisia, Spain and along the coast of France. The Etruscans travelled northwards, as well, across the Alps and into the European wilderness in search of amber, tin and iron. There, they set up trade with native Celts and Gauls, exchanging bags of salt or their beautifully wrought bronze objects for raw materials. Etruscan styles of dress and armor were copied by these northern tribes, as were Etruscan symbols of power. The runic alphabets of Germany and Scandinavia are even believed to have been derived from the Etruscan alphabet. The German word for metal, *erz*, may be linked to traders from the Etruscan town of Arezzo. For several hundred years, Etruscan wine was famous: it was even exported to France.

Like the Romans after them, the Etruscans were remarkably open to the influences of other cultures. The Phoenicians, the Greeks and the Carthaginians all had important commercial and military ties with Etruscan cities, and the Etruscans adopted many elements of these foreign cultures into their own. The first flourishing of Etruscan art is known as the orientalizing period, because the Etruscans incorporated so many Near Eastern images and themes into their own works. Lions and palm fronds decorate Etruscan mirrors and vases. Etruscan clothing, which would later be adopted by Rome, was modelled after Near Eastern styles. Greek settlers in Italy probably gave the Etruscans their writing systems. Etruscans loved Greek mythology, and made many Greek myths their own. They enjoyed and appreciated art. Not only did they make beautiful things themselves, they were also avid collectors. Numerous examples of oriental vases, Egyptian faïence, and Assyrian ivories have been found in Etruscan tombs. Etruscans were particularly fond of Greek art. In fact, the Etruscans were such good collectors of things Greek, more examples of Greek vases have been unearthed in excavations in Etruria than have been found in all of Greece.

Everything we know about the Etruscans tells us that they were a happy people who knew how to enjoy themselves and appreciated the finer things in life. Much of our understanding of Etruscan ways comes from paintings found in their tombs, many of which have been discovered in the last two centuries. Murals on tomb walls show them dancing and dining, hunting and fishing, or participating in athletic contests. Scenes of Etruscan life frequently depict a musician playing on twin pipes while naked entertainers dance for a party of revellers. Contemporaries of the Etruscans wrote that they were so fond of music they would do nothing without its accompaniment, and musicians, who were probably slaves, played to them while they ate, worked, went to sleep, went to war, and even while they cooked and hunted. A Roman writer of the third century BC described an Etruscan hunting party in which music was used to lure the wild beasts into the open:

> Nets are stretched out, and all kinds of traps are set into position in a circle. A skilled flutist then plays the sweetest tunes the double flute can produce, avoiding the shriller notes. The quiet and the stillness carry the sounds, and the music floats up into all the lairs and resting places of the animals. At first the animals are terrified. But later they are irresistibly overcome by the enjoyment of the music. Spellbound, they are gradually attracted by the powerful music and, forgetting their young and their homes, they draw near, bewitched by the sounds, until they fall, overpowered by the melody, into the snares.

Etruscan musicians were well known for their skill, and the sweetness of Etruscan melodies doubtless contributed to the idea that the Etruscans were a sensuous and a pleasure loving people. They were unusually rich, and both the men and the women adorned themselves with what, to the more conservative Romans, seemed an excessive amount of expensive jewelry. They were famous for their special hinged shoes, which were in much demand throughout the Mediterranean, and they were greedy importers of all manner of sumptuous fabric. Their fame for luxurious living made then seem suspiciously decadent in early Roman and Greek eyes: the Etruscans lived so well and enjoyed themselves so thoroughly they shocked their more prudish contemporaries. Roman and Greek writers tell us that the Etruscan men were fat, cruel, and without morals, and that the women were exhibitionists and prostitutes. The Etruscans were famous for their banqueting parties, at which huge amounts of food and drink were consumed while dancers and musicians entertained the guests. These parties were particularly shocking to the Greeks because Etruscan couples dined together, even lying on the same coach. The ancient Greeks believed in a strict separation of the sexes: no Greek banqueting party would include women - except, of course, for slave girls, who were purely entertainment. One Greek writer, appalled by what he saw in Etruria, describes Etruscan society this way:

> . . . it is normal for the Etruscans to share their women in common. These women take great care of their bodies and exercise bare, exposing their bodies even before men, and among themselves: for it is not shameful for them to appear almost naked.. . .they dine not with their husbands, but with any man who happens to be present; and they toast anyone they want to.
>
> And the Etruscans raise all the children that are born, not knowing who the father is of each one. The children also eventually live like those who brought them up, and have many drinking parties, and they too make love with all the women.
>
> It is no shame for Etruscans to be seen having sexual experiences. . . for this too is normal: it is the local custom there. And so far are they from considering it shameful that they even say, when the master of the house is making love, and someone asks for him, that he is "involved in such and such," shamelessly calling out the thing by name.

The composer of these lines was not, of course, an objective historian. The Etruscans had a happier way of life than any of their contemporaries on the Italian peninsula, but there is no evidence that they lacked social or family structure or that they were advocates of free love. Actually, the scandalized attitude of this description probably reflects the fact that the Etruscan women lived much freer lives than any of their contemporaries. At the height of Etruscan civilization, during the sixth century BC, Roman women were still largely confined to the house. Like Greek women, they were not welcome at evening parties. They ate separately, and laws prohibited them from drinking alcoholic beverages at all. It was customary for the women of a Roman household to kiss the pater familias on the cheek every day, not as an expression of affection, but so that he could tell if she had been drinking.

By contrast, Etruscan women were treated as the social, if not as the political equals of their brothers and husbands. Not only did they attend banquets at which they ate and drank as much as they liked, they also walked unescorted on the streets and freely attended public spectacles. Paintings on tomb walls show that women were present at horse races, wrestling matches, plays and dances. Unlike early Roman women, they also had their own names (Roman women's names were derived from the names of their fathers until they were married and from the names of their husbands afterward), and were legally capable of holding their own property. Etruscan married couples went about together, and might even display physical affection in public. Etruscan art shows that their society was one of couples, and that older women sometimes took up with younger men. Decorative bronze mirrors depict men and women playing dice or board games with one another; yet another departure from standard practice since Greek and Roman women were strictly enjoined from sitting down at the gaming table. One particularly interesting mirror shows a young man and woman about to start a game, accompanied by a few lines of dialogue: "I'm going to beat you," she says. "I do believe you are," he replies.

The strength of Etruscan women is evident in the story which grew up around Tarquin, the first Etruscan king of Rome. Tarquin came from Tarquinia, the oldest of the Etruscan cities. According to the story, he left Tarquinia under the encouragement of his wife, Tanaquil, who believed he was destined for greatness in Rome. Tanaquil is said to have helped him rise to power, and, after he became king, legend tells us she picked his successor, her son-in-law, Servius Tullius. But Tanaquil was not the only strong woman in the Tarquin family. Tullia, Servius Tullius's daughter, found herself married to the weaker of two Tarquin brothers. Tullia's sister was married to the stronger brother: Lucius Tarquinius, a man destined, perhaps, to be king. Tullia felt that she would be a better wife for this man than her weaker sister. The sister, according to Tullia, lacked *muliebris audacia*: "the daring proper to a woman". Apparently, Lucius agreed with Tullia's feelings on this matter. Graphically demonstrating that *she* was not lacking muliebris audacia, Tullia killed her weak husband as well as her sister, and married Lucius. She then pushed him into seizing the throne, and actually drove a chariot over the body of her own father in the process. The site of this dreadful crime was a Roman street which ever after bore the name Sceleratus Vicus: the street of horrors.

Evidently, one of the things which distinguished the Etruscans was their passion. The Etruscans apparently lived life to the fullest, well aware both of earthly pleasures and of earthly pains. Their most compelling art is lively and gay. Scenes from a tomb known as the "Hunting and Fishing Tomb" portray the pleasures of upper class Etruscan life. A smiling, naked figure dives head first into a blue sea is populated by dolphins and fish. Overhead, flocks of multi-colored birds fly about, unaware of the hunter who aims his slingshot at them. In another room, two young men ride back from the hunt on their horses, accompanied by a servant who holds their dogs on a leash, and other servants who carry back their game on a pole. Different tombs show scenes of banquets and revelry, horse races and outdoor sports, as well as scenes taken from Greek mythology. Although the colors of these paintings have faded considerably, the scenes still throb with a gay and exuberant vitality.

But the imaginative vigor of the Etruscans was a double edged sword. Later Etruscan painting displays a distinct preoccupation with the dark forces of nature: with hideous beasts, demons and death. In the Tomb of the Underworld, a beautiful girl confronts Charu, the Etruscan God who will lead her soul on its final journey downward. He is a horrific vision: his greenish skin is mottled with decay, his red eyes blaze above his beak-like nose, twisting snakes hiss from his tangled hair. The Underworld in this tomb seethes with demons, vultures and snakes. In the next room, the King and Queen of Hell await their victim: his helmet is a wolf's head with wide open jaws; her crown is a throng of swirling snakes. Other tombs show the more violent enjoyments of Etruria. The Etruscan reputation for cruelty may have come from a taste for bloody spectacles: paintings of slaves fighting with animals suggest that gladiatorial games were an Etruscan invention. Certain other features of Etruscan art indicate they may have practiced human sacrifice: some scenes show blood, dismembered arms, legs, and severed heads.

The Etruscans excelled at metal work and sculpture as well as at painting. Again, most of our samples of Etruscan genius are taken from funerary art. Statues and reliefs from tombs show remarkably natural techniques of portraying the human body, as well as a concern for the individuality of each subject. While Greek sculpture tended to idealize the human form, Etruscan sculpture showed people as they really were. Etruscan sculpture also conveyed more warmth and interpersonal emotion than Greek sculpture. Tomb scenes of graceful married couples, lounging in each other's arms for eternity, show the Etruscan belief in human attachment. Scenes of mothers with children emphasize the importance of family life. Some of the most fascinating Etruscan art works are those showing mythical beasts. A bronze statue of a chimaera - a creature with the body of a lion, a goat's head growing from its shoulders, and a serpent for a tail - snarls out over the centuries. A pair of horses, harnessed and straining forward, hold their plumed wings erect behind them. Even the famous statue of the wolf which suckles Romulus and Remus on the Captoline Hill, symbol for Rome, was probably made by an Etruscan sculptor. The twin boys of the statue were added to the Etruscan original during the Renaissance, but ancient Roman references tell us that, in its ancient form, the boys were a part of the scene.

The Etruscans were a highly religious and superstitious people, well known for their skill in interpreting omens. Like many ancient people, the Etruscans believed that the gods made their will known to men by the means of various natural signs. The Etruscans divided these signs into three categories. Priests were trained to read the meaning of patterns of lightning, the flights of birds, and finally the disposition of the entrails of slaughtered animals. Etruscan priests devised a whole science of how to interpret signs and wrote about them in religious books which made up a body of literature called the Etrusca Disciplina. These Etruscan books were widely read, not just by the Etruscans, but by the Romans as well, who relied upon Etruscan priests to help them communicate with the gods. The examiners of entrails were called haruspices, lightning observers were fulgiatores, and bird watchers were augures. One of the more famous examples of Etruscan art is a bronze model of a liver which was found in Piacenza. This liver was a teaching device which was marked to show which gods displayed themselves in the various areas of the organ.

In the later days of Rome, the Etrusca Disciplina were translated into Latin and apparently used to make up a part of every Roman boy's education. Even after the rise of Rome and the virtual destruction of Etruscan civilization, Etruscan priests still played important roles in Roman culture. The Emperor Augustus regularly consulted his haruspices. Etruscan religious rites were adopted by the Romans to consecrate their cities, to sanctify their temples. and to ensure their victories at war. The religious rite which marked the founding of the city of Rome was probably also an Etruscan ritual, and it was probably presided over by Etruscan priests. Elements of Etruscan beliefs and practices survived for a long time after the Etruscan people themselves were gone and forgotten. The Romans probably inherited the twelve month calendar from Etruscan priests: the number twelve was especially significant in Etruscan religion. Many Roman divinities were taken from the Etruscan pantheon, and the art of astrology came directly from the Etruscans.

Although one does not necessarily have to believe that the Etruscans actually had the power to read the will of the gods, it is nonetheless true that some of their predictions were uncannily accurate. The Etruscans believed that races of people were destined to rule the earth for certain prescribed periods of time, after which they were fated to perish. They predicted that their own era of predominance, which began in the tenth century BC, would last until the beginning of the first century. By the beginning of the Christian era, Etruscan civilization was, indeed, no more. The old story of Romulus founding Rome has him seeing an omen of twelve birds landing upon the Palatine Hill. Etruscan augures claimed that this meant that Rome would last for twelve *saeculae*. If a secula was one hundred years, and Rome was founded in 753 BC, then, according to the prophecy, Rome's power would last until 447 AD. Although the fall of Rome, marked by the invasion of Alaric the Goth occurred in 410, weak Emperors officially ruled Rome until 476, after which point the power of the Roman people vanished. Ironically enough, the last Roman Emperor, who was removed from power by the barbarian king Odoacer, like the first Roman king, bore the name Romulus.

[69]

Although we know a great deal about the Etrusca Disciplina from hints dropped by ancient Roman writers, no example of the books themselves, either in the original Etruscan or in Latin translation has ever been found. In fact, although the Etruscans apparently had an extensive national literature, which included religious books, histories, poems and plays, not one single important Etruscan text has been found. Almost ten thousand fragments of Etruscan writing have been uncovered, but no long works and no extended bilingual texts number among these fragments. Thus we do not know the character of Etruscan literature, and we cannot learn about the Etruscan life from an insider's point of view.

Not only does the lack of Etruscan literature prevent us from gaining an understanding of the details of Etruscan higher culture, it also prevents us from knowing some of the most fundamental facts about the history and the origin of the people themselves. Because of the fragmentary nature of the Etruscan writing that we do have, nobody has yet been able to completely decipher their language. The Etruscans used an alphabet derived from archaic Greek, and because of this, Etruscan words can be pronounced. As one scholar put the problem "Reading Etruscan is not difficult. The problem is to understand what is being read." We know many Etruscan place names, some of which survive in a modified form, and we know the names of a long list of Etruscan gods: twenty eight of them are cited on the Piacenza liver alone. We also know a few common names, as well as some rudiments of grammar, and a list of words from the tombs. But, because we do not have any longer texts in Etruscan, the structure of their language remains poorly understood, and linguists have been unable to determine which language group Etruscan belongs to.

If the first mystery of the Etruscans is their language, the second is their origin. The question of who the Etruscans were and where they came from has been a matter of debate ever since the first references were made to them in the fifth century BC. No doubt because of the relatively advanced and distinctive nature of their civilization, coupled with their taste for Eastern styles and foreign goods, many people are convinced that the Etruscan civilization did not grow up on Italian soil. Because of their undeniable cultural links to the Near East, many historians have claimed that the Etruscans were a transplanted race, made up of refugees from an overpopulated land.

The first historian to recount the tale of the Etruscan people was the Greek writer Herodotus. Herodotus claimed that the Etruscans were descendants of people from Asia Minor called the Lydians. According to Herodotus, whose source was a very proud Lydian writer named Xanthus, a great drought and famine plagued Lydia for eighteen years. The people bore the scarcity of food with patience, inventing hundreds of games, such as dice, knucklebones, and ball to distract themselves from their hunger. They would eat every other day, playing games on the alternate day "so that they would not have to eat." Finally, Atys, King of Lydia, decreed that half the population would have to go to live elsewhere:

> He appointed himself to rule the section whose lot determined they should remain, and his son Tyrrhenus to command the emigrants. The lots were drawn, and one section went down the coast of Smyrna, where they built vessels, put aboard all their household effects and sailed in search of livelihood elsewhere. They passed many countries and finally reached Umbria in the north of Italy, where they settled and still live to this day. Here they changed their name from Lydians to Tyrrhenians after the king's son Tyrrhenus, who was their leader.

The story of the Lydian exodus is no doubt a romantic one, and throughout history, many people have claimed that it definitively solves the Etruscan mystery. The ancient Greeks (and even some modern writers) refer to Etruscans as the Tyrrhenians, and seem to accept the Lydian story as an objective historical report. Of course, like the tale of Romulus and Remus, this is a legend with many fanciful elements, some blatantly incorrect information, and at least a hint of nationalistic propaganda. For instance, the Etruscans never seemed to have called themselves Tyrrhenians. They referred to themselves as Rasenna. The King Atys, in the legend, is supposed to be the son of Manes, the first man.

Xanthus, the Lydian source of the story, proudly considers his own country to be the cradle of not just the Etruscans, but of the human race as well. The story also neatly explains the origin of board games, which were in fact popular among the Etruscans, although one might wonder what kind of game would successfully replace dinner in a starving country.

Although many ancient and modern people believed the Lydian story, it was far from being universally accepted. Another Greek writer, Dionysius of Halicarnassus, writing four centuries after Herodotus, claimed that the Etruscans were an indigenous Italian population. He pointed out, among other things, that Herodotus himself could not have believed the tale of the Lydians since he also described the Etruscans as descendants of Phoecaean Greeks. Furthermore, he said, Etruscan cultural links with the Lydian people were quite negligible:

> I do not believe that the Tyrrhenians were a colony of Lydians. For they do not use the same language as the latter, nor can it be alleged that, though they no longer speak a similar tongue, they nevertheless still retain some other indications of their mother country. For they neither worship the same gods as the Lydians, nor make use of similar laws or institutions.

Although the possibility remains open that the earliest Etruscan settlers in Italy did come from the Near East, most modern scholars consider the Etruscan people to be as much a native Italian population as the Romans themselves. Like the Romans, the Etruscans blossomed when they came into contact with Greek and Near Eastern culture, and like the Romans, they incorporated many foreign elements into their own art and society. Ancient records reveal that the Etruscans were also unusually open to foreigners, and that, in all likelihood, many immigrants to Etruria became Etruscan citizens. Whether or not the ancient, prehistoric tribes which would become the Etruscans were a migratory population from somewhere else is a different question entirely. Etruscan civilization was unique: it was not a division of some other, larger and early civilization. Although the Etruscans developed at a rapid rate, their evolution took place on the Italian peninsula. The Etruscan *culture* is therefore conclusively Italian, just as American culture is American, even though it owes debts to thousands of outside influences.

Etruscan domination of Rome itself ended in the year 510 BC, when the last Etruscan king was allegedly thrown out of the city. This last king was called Tarquinius Superbus (Tarquin the Arrogant), and he was reportedly a proud, cruel and despotic leader. In fact, Roman historians tell us he was such an autocratic and self-willed tyrant, the Roman people made up their minds never to be ruled by kings again. Instead, they set up a Republic, presided over by a body of patrician leaders called the Senate, who were in turn under the guidance of two elected heads of state called Consuls. Of course, the Roman resolution never again to have a king was pretty well broken five centuries later when the Republic, ruled by the Senate and the Consuls, evolved into the Empire, commanded by the Emperor.

After the expulsion of Tarquin the Arrogant, the Romans and the Etruscan States were more or less at war with one another. Although the Etruscan civilization was culturally advanced, the Etruscans were not politically aware. The twelve major Etruscan cities, while they had linguistic, artistic and religious unity, never united to form a nation, but remained autonomous city states. Because they did not work together to protect themselves from Roman expansion, Roman armies eventually overcame every Etruscan city, and these cities were more or less thoroughly Romanized. Many people may still argue about where the Etruscans came from, but most people agree that sometime during the first centuries before and after Christ, Etruscan civilization disappeared. It is no mystery, however what became of the Etruscans. They became the Romans.

Even with the disappearance of the people themselves, Etruscan influence lingers on. As the Roman civilization evolved, it incorporated many Etruscan elements. The luxurious Etruscan banquet became a Roman custom, and, according to all reports, the Romans enjoyed themselves at least as much as the Etruscans. The Etruscan taste for lavish displays of wealth, elaborate shows and imaginative spectacles became a Roman trademark. The relatively

[73]

liberated position of Etruscan women was adopted by the more repressed Roman matron. The typical Etruscan piece of clothing, the tebenna, became the Roman toga. And finally, the Etruscan principles of engineering and architecture were the basis for the construction of grand Roman edifices all over the Empire. Etruscans were true Italians, and their contributions to the Roman-Italian culture were immeasurable.

To this day, Italy still feels an Etruscan presence. The area which the Etruscans once dominated in northern Italy, now called Tuscany, is still sometimes referred to as Etruria. Many of Italy's greatest artistic and creative geniuses came out of Tuscany, such as Leonardo da Vinci, Michelangelo, Giotto and Dante. Great twentieth century artists, such as the sculptor Giacometti, create works of art inspired by Etruscan originals. Enzo Ferrari, creator of the world's greatest sports car, came from Tuscany, as did the fashion designers Gucci and Giorgio Armani. Although the people of Tuscany may not have literally descended from Etruscan stock, they did inherit an Etruscan cultural legacy. Some linguists believe that the softer accent of the Italian spoken by Tuscan people might echo ancient Etruscan speech patterns. The English writer, D.H. Lawrence, who explored the Etruscan tombs early in our century remarked on the survival of Etruscan ways; "How much more Etruscan than Roman the Italian of today is: sensitive, diffident, craving really for symbols and mysteries, able to be delighted with true delight over small things, violent in spasms, and altogether without sternness or natural will-to-power." Because we do not know the whole story of the Etruscans, because their history and their literature has been lost, we cannot measure the true extent of their importance and their influence on the customs and achievements of the ancient Mediterranean world. We do know however, that their contributions to civilization fertilized the Italian soil. We can be sure that although the people themselves are lost, their influence will never vanish.

CHAPTER FOUR

A Christian World

Dominus pascit me: nihil mihi deest;
In pascuis virentibus cubare me facit.
Ad aquas, ubi quiescam, conducit me;
Reficit animam meam.
Deducit me per semitas rectas
Propter nomen suum.

--The 23rd Psalm

Whether or not we consider ourselves to be Christians, the world we live in today is a Christian world. For the past sixteen hundred years, Christianity has been a dominant force in the political, literary, artistic and personal life of America and of European nations. In all of its many forms, Christianity is the largest organized religion in the world. According to the 1994 World Almanac, almost two billion people consider themselves to be Christian. The next most popular religion, Islam, has fewer than one billion adherents. Two hundred and thirty nine million Christians live in North America alone. Although Christianity did not originate in Italy, it owes much of its success to the Roman Empire. Initially, Rome resisted the Christians, who were considered enemies of the state. Christians were persecuted, tortured, sent into gladiatorial rings, and murdered outright by emissaries of the hostile Emperors. However, during the fourth century, one of the greatest turnarounds on history occurred: the Roman Emperor himself became a Christian. Soon thereafter, Christianity was adopted as the official state religion and the state itself helped to spread the gospel throughout the realm.

After the end of Imperial rule, the Christian church used the structure of the Roman Empire to govern its people. Like the Empire itself, Christianity made its headquarters in Rome. Long after the decline of Roman political power, Roman spiritual power held sway over the Western world. The Christian church preserved many Roman customs as well as works of art and literature which would certainly have been lost if Christian monks and scholars had not treasured them. In this way, the Christian church derived much of its strength from Rome, and, in return, made sure that Roman achievements would live to enrich our culture for generations to come. In addition, a vast Christian culture, inspired in large part by Italian monks, artists, and thinkers transformed medieval Europe. Soaring cathedrals, resplendent with stained glass windows and glittering with mosaic tile grew up throughout the ancient Roman lands. Pilgrims made their way to Rome from all over the Christian world, some of them travelling on original Roman roads. The political unity of Europe gave way to a spiritual unity: a unity which, in modified form, exists even today. The Roman Empire prepared the ground for Christianity, and Christianity took full advantage of the Empire's vast, though decaying resources.

The Roman Empire was not, of course, always a friend to the Christian church. Nor was the Christian church always a friend to the Roman Empire. Some historians, like Edward Gibbon, even blame Christianity and the Christians for the Empire's downfall. During the first three centuries of the Christian era, Rome, sensing its peril, was bent on obliterating Christianity altogether. For three hundred years, torturing and killing Christian believers seemed to be a Roman national sport.

> . . . Blandina was filled with such a power that those who took turns torturing her morning and night were exhausted and finally gave up. They were amazed she could still breath. But Blandina grew in strength as she proclaimed her faith, saying, "I am a Christian, we do nothing to be ashamed of."

Blandina, a homely servant woman living in Gaul during the second century, was an enemy of the Roman state. She was first tortured and then sent to the arena to face the wild beasts. When even they failed to kill her, she was finally put to death by a gladiator. The Roman spectators of the grisly performance admitted that "never yet had they known a woman suffer so much or so long." Blandina's only crime, as she herself said, was that she was a Christian.

Blandina was alone neither in her faith nor in her fate. Thousands of Christians died for their belief, some of them, like Blandina, publicly executed in gruesome gladiatorial shows. Christians, considered criminals for three hundred years, were sporadically singled out by the government for systematic elimination. The first and most famous of these organized persecutions occurred in 64 AD during the reign of the infamous Emperor Nero. After a catastrophic fire which destroyed much of Rome, Nero accused Rome's Christian community of arson. He had hundreds of Christians arrested, convicted, and put to death. Many people believed that it was Nero himself who set the fire, and that he was simply using Christians, whose religious practices were widely regarded with suspicion, as convenient scapegoats.

One might wonder why the Romans, who were generally a tolerant people, would be so intolerant of Christianity. After all, for hundreds of years, the Roman Empire had coexisted peacefully with any number of different religions, and, because of the Romans' peculiar ability to adapt elements of foreign cultures into their own, any one city in the Empire might contain adherents to a wide variety of religious sects. However, there was one compelling reason for which the Roman government felt that Christians were a dangerous and a subversive people. Because Christianity is a strictly monotheistic religion whose writings specifically forbid the worship of other gods, the Christians would not make sacrifices to the Emperor. Since they refused to honor the Emperor, they were deemed traitors to the State and even atheists, whose very presence was a threat to the stability of the Empire.

Since Christianity was not officially tolerated by the State, many Christians met and worshipped in secret. Some histories claim that early Christians were forced to practice their religion literally underground in the catacombs beneath the city. While this story is only a myth, the actual practices of Christians were not widely understood by the general populace. According to some rumors, Christians performed barbaric rites, such as drinking human blood and eating the flesh of babies. Those who were actually acquainted with Christians were generally impressed by their piety, self-control and altruism. Even emperors hostile to the Christians, such as Julian the Apostate, were struck by their charity. In an attempt to bring people back into the pagan temples, he tried to encourage his priests to learn from the example of the Christians:

> Why do we not observe that it is their benevolence to stran-gers, their care for the graves of the dead and the pretended holiness of their lives that has done the most to increase atheism [Christianity]? . . . let us not, by allowing others to out-do us in good works, disgrace by such remissness, or rather, utterly abandon, reverence due to the Gods.

Fortunately for the Christians, official persecutions were only sporadically carried out against them. Large numbers of people were born to live, worship and die as Christians without once en-countering even a grain of opposition from the government. Because the Christians were good citizens, who could be relied upon to live orderly lives and to pay their taxes, they were not always considered enemies of the Roman State. But when Rome did decide to persecute them, the punishments were severe, and usually ended in death. People who were accused of being Chris-tians could be cleared of the crime by one simple act; all they had to do was offer sacrifice to the Emperor and they could go free. The Emperor Trajan, who ruled from 98 to 117, wrote that Chris-tians must be punished unless "the party denies himself to be a Christian, and shall give proof that he is not (that is, by adoring our Gods)" in which case "he shall be pardoned on ground of repentance." Trajan's rationale for this policy was that any true Christian could not be made to sacrifice to pagan gods, no matter how severe the torture or how great his pain. Although it is cer-tainly true that many people who practiced Christianity were neither ready nor willing to die for it, hundreds of suffering martyrs seem to prove that Trajan was right.

One particularly impressive Christian martyr was a woman from Carthage called Perpetua, a lady of noble birth who lived during the reign of Septimus Severus (193-211). Around the year 200, persecution broke out against the Christians, and she was arrested and incarcerated, along with her friends and servants. She was twenty two at the time, married, and nursing an infant son. An intelligent and well-educated woman, she wrote an account of what happened to her during her time in prison, and her story is probably the earliest extant Christian document written by a woman. She describes how her father came to her day after day, begging her, pleading with her to renounce her Christian faith and thus save her life and the life of her baby. He kissed her hands and threw himself at her feet, entreating her to make a sacrifice to the Emperor and be allowed to live.

But Perpetua could not be moved: she saw her destiny clearly, and calmly accepted her fate. At the tribunal she was given one last chance to save herself; even the governor tried to reason with her, to persuade her to "have pity on your father's grey head; have pity on your infant son." But Perpetua was true to her religion, and despite all entreaties, she persisted in asserting that she was a Christian. Along with her companions, Perpetua was sentenced to be thrown to the beasts. She writes that after the sentencing "we returned to the prison in high spirits."

Perpetua and her companions were killed in the amphitheater of Carthage at a public spectacle. Witnesses to such martyrdoms marvelled at the strength of the Christian faith which enabled its followers to undergo a multitude of tortures for its sake. The suffering of these early martyrs, far from discouraging people from becoming Christians, helped to swell the ranks of Christ's followers. A religion which could elicit such unswerving devotion, which allowed its adherents to face death unafraid, impressed and captivated many Romans. One of the reasons that Christianity gained so many followers was that it offered not simply a new belief system, but a whole way of life. Far more than just a cult which gave people a new God, Christianity instructed people on how to live a pure and a good life, stressing community values and altruism. Christianity freed its followers from the fear of superstitions; God would accept anybody who accepted him, and was not, like the old gods of Greece and Rome, a temperamental, capricious creature who might decide to destroy one's life on a whim.

Another reason that Christianity gained such a strong foothold during its early days, was that it was a religion that accepted and appealed to the underclasses and to women. Early Christian teaching held that all men and women were made in God's image and were equal before his eyes. Thus, in God's kingdom, the slave was the equal of his master, the woman the equal of her husband. It is little wonder then, that Christianity caught on quickly among the many slaves in the Empire. Women, too, were allowed an unprecedentedly large role in the Christian Church. Although there is much debate on exactly how powerful women were, there is no doubt that many followers of Christ were female - indeed, according to the gospels, women were the last people to leave the cross after the Crucifixion, and it was to women that Christ first appeared after the Resurrection. A Christian woman was expected to administer to the poor and the needy and was allowed to go about the business of charity. Early Christian women were teachers and even, some argue, bishops in the church. Christian moral teaching also attempted to give women some stability in their personal lives by making adultery a sin; a Christian woman married to a Christian man did not have to worry about her husband deserting her for one of his concubines.

In fact, Christianity was not simply a new religious system, it was a real social and political revolution. Anybody who wonders that the mere admission of Christianity was enough to condemn an otherwise law abiding citizen to death, need only consider what Christian teaching says about the equal value of all human life. By refusing to worship the emperor as a god, the Christian was challenging the entire Roman system. He was saying that the emperor was no better than he was. He was even saying that the emperor was no better than the lowliest slave in the city or the least unwanted baby, abandoned to die in a trash heap. By giving value to all human life, the Christian was denying the moral rightness of the Roman political and social system. Some Christians even went so far as to claim that the pagan gods which the emperor worshipped were actually demons, whose only purpose was to trick him and lead him away from the true path of righteousness. Because of this, a Christian was indeed a dangerous and a subversive person.

Despite the tortures and the persecutions, Christianity spread throughout the Mediterranean world, and, by the beginning of the fourth century, it is estimated that about one tenth of the Roman Empire was Christian. The last persecution was carried out by the Emperor Diocletian. Called the Great Persecution, it began in the year 303. During this period, which was one of systematic destruction of churches and slaughter of believers, the Roman mint struck coins commemorating the "annihilation of the Christians." But these coins were only wishful thinking on the part of the Emperor: the Christians were rapidly gaining strength and numbers. The strength that Christianity was gathering to itself was not simply numerical, it was political as well. An important convert to Christianity was a woman named Helena, the mother of a man named Constantine. Constantine would succeed Diocletian as Emperor, and, following his mother, he too would become a Christian.

The exact time and the actual cause of Constantine's conversion are open to debate. Before his conversion, Constantine was probably an adherent of a popular religion of the time called mithraism. Mithraism originated in Persia and spread westward, into Rome, where it caught on, particularly among the military classes. The religion worshipped a sun-god named Mithra, and, at least superficially, had much in common with Christianity, both in its practices and in its belief system. Although mithraism was Christianity's strongest rival - Diocletian, who was known to be a mithraic, proclaimed Mithra the "protector of the Empire" - the religion was not destined for greatness, partly because it lacked a central organization and partly because it excluded women almost entirely.

Prior to his conversion, Constantine fought under a banner which depicted the sun, appealing to the power of Mithra. In 312 A.D., he came to Rome to reclaim the Empire from Maxentius, a would-be usurper. Perhaps at the instigation of his mother, he had a cross painted on his banner and upon the shields of his soldiers as well. Just before his final battle with Maxentius at the Milvian

[81]

bridge in Rome, he claims to have seen the vision of the cross superimposed upon the sun - a clear sign that divine aid could come from one source alone. Constantine won the battle in a rout, and Maxentius was killed. Thereafter, Constantine threw off whatever vestiges of mithraic belief he still adhered to, and saw himself as the chosen servant of the "Highest Divinity." To the Christian community, the unthinkable had occurred: a Roman Emperor had become a Christian.

The effects of Constantine's conversion were many and widespread. In fact, one must imagine that the world we live in today would be a far different place if Constantine had never become a Christian. Soon after his conversion, in 313 A.D., he issued a declaration, known as the Edict of Milan, which called for the toleration of all religions in the Empire, and thus officially ended the persecutions. He renounced his role as god on earth and no longer required that religious sacrifices be made to him. He donated an opulent palace to be the home of the bishop of Rome. He exempted Christian churches from paying taxes, and granted favors to members of the clergy. In 321, he issued another edict which forbade work on Sunday, the day of the Lord. The tide had turned for the Christians; no longer outlaws, they were now the favorites of the state. Christians living during the early fourth century must have been astounded and overwhelmed by their sudden change of fortune.

A few years after Constantine's death, his nephew Julian took the throne. Julian is called "the Apostate" because, nostalgic for the old order of the Empire, he reversed the Edict of Milan and tried to re-institute pagan religions. He had little success, however. Once people turned to Christianity, there was no turning them back. As one writer noted it is "easier to write letters on the surface of a pool of water" than to reconvert Christians; "the liquid closes over every stroke." Julian's other mission as emperor was to reclaim lands in Asia Minor which had fallen to invaders. Leading his armies on a campaign, he was killed in battle just three years after coming into power.

From the death of Julian onwards, Christianity began to play a larger and larger role in the social and political life of the declining empire. In 371, Emperor Theodosius declared Christianity the official state religion and ordered all Romans to become Christian. The bishop of Rome, who was regarded as the head of all the bishops in the church, took on greater importance and came to be known as the Pontifex Maximus. The church borrowed the hierarchical structure of the Roman Empire to administer its spiritual domain, which now extended throughout and beyond the area of the Empire at its height. As the political and military influence of Rome disintegrated, the power of the religion centered in Rome grew. Although the Romans did not invent Christianity, it was through Roman channels and Roman politics that the religion was able to overtake the entire European continent.

The fifth century is known as the time of the Germanic migrations. The migrations actually began in around 375 A.D., when the Asiatic Huns began to invade German lands, forcing the Germans to seek refuge elsewhere. Great waves of Germanic tribes came out of the North and East and began to infiltrate and conquer the old Roman lands. In 410, a tribe called the Visigoths invaded Italy and sacked Rome. Rome, in decline for many years, was no longer the ruler of the western world, and her armies could not defend the borders of the lands she once held. Germanic tribes invaded England, France and Spain, and Roman civilization was engulfed in the tides of barbarianism. Despite the Germanic invasions, Roman culture was not wholly lost. In many places, the Germans preserved Roman laws and customs, and some German kings even took an interest in Roman philosophy. Furthermore, the Roman Empire, which had earlier been divided into an Eastern and a Western half, continued to flourish in the West, where, from its center in Constantinople, it carried on Roman traditions and Roman ways of life until the fifteenth century.

The single most important factor in the survival of the Roman civilization was the Christian church, which, even during the chaotic time of the German invasions, grew more and more powerful. The supremacy of the Roman pope was affirmed by Pope Leo the Great in the middle of the fifth century. The pope began as the ruler of the church, but soon gained enough political power that kings and emperors deferred to him. The pope was emperor, the bishops were generals, and the common people were foot soldiers in God's army.

The power of Christianity was not just political; it affected all aspects of medieval life. Some of the greatest thinkers and philosophers of all time were Christian theologians, who wrote their works in Latin from within the sanctuary of the church. The church preserved and promoted scholarship, and was responsible for the survival of many great pre-Christian Italian works of literature, as well as for the continued importance of the Latin language. St. Jerome, a classical scholar of the fifth century, translated the Old and New Testaments from their original Hebrew and Greek into Latin. His version of the Bible, known as the Vulgate, was still used well into the twentieth century. Medieval scholars appreciated the greatness of pagan Roman authors, and kept copies of their works to study them. The church was an oasis of high culture during the Middle Ages, a place where the greatest literary and philosophical accomplishments of the early Italians lived on, and continued to shape the minds and the ideas of the people.

Christianity profoundly affected the course of Western history, in artistic, literary and political terms. A very large percentage of our greatest works of literature make references to Christian stories. An even larger percentage of paintings and statues portray Christian themes and Christian heroes. During the Middle Ages, some of the greatest works of art were the decorations in the churches, which showed scenes from the life of Christ or the lives of the saints. Some of the best illustrations of this kind are in the medieval churches of Italy, which are decorated with elaborate and beautiful mosaics. The most impressive mosaics can be found within the churches of Ravenna, which, for a time after the fall of Rome, was considered the capital of the Italian Empire. Housed within modest and austere-looking brick buildings, the mosaic scenes which line the interior walls dazzle the visitor with their splendor. Each mosaic is composed of thousands of cubes of glass, marble, enamel and sometimes mother-of pearl, which catch and reflect and multiply the light as it hits them, filling the churches with a shimmering aura of luminescent brilliance. An unknown Latin poet, writing of one of these churches, said "Either light was born here, or imprisoned here, it reigns supreme."

The churches of the Middle Ages were not only the literary

and artistic centers of Europe, they were also the social and moral centers. The vast majority of common folk in Europe considered themselves Christians, and most of them received some kind of instruction and guidance from the church, whether by attending mass, getting married, having their children baptized, or receiving their last rites. The Church was a great unifier of medieval communities, which, although it differed slightly from country to country, delivered a similar message and a similar philosophy of living to people from Ireland to the Russian steppe. In fact, the Roman Church probably ruled people's lives more strictly than the Roman Empire ever did, since it affected every aspect of human existence, from birth to procreation, right on to death. During periods of political upheaval, the church remained strong, safe and the same; it was the one true unified system left after the downfall of the Empire.

In terms of cultural leadership, the Christian church carried on where the Romans left off. More than anything else, it was the Christian church which was responsible for the continued survival of Italian culture throughout Europe. The church preserved the glowing remnants of Roman culture, and offered them to the invading Germanic tribes. Some tribes were already Christian when they came to Roman lands, others converted to Christianity. Some Christian writers who witnessed the final disintegration of Roman power thought that the fall of the Empire was a good thing since it offered the chance to lead barbarians to salvation. The new rulers of old Roman lands relied on the bishops and other leaders within the church to help them administer their domain. Once the Roman school systems were no more, the men of the church were often the only people left who could read and write: they were invaluable to the frequently illiterate new kings.

Despite political upheavals, despite the warring kings and separate tribes, an Italian influence still united Europe. From as far away as Ireland, which had never been a part of the Roman system, rulers, kings and religious leaders looked to Italy for guidance. The Empire still existed, stronger than ever, only now it was a holy, spiritual empire, which bound the people to it through moral and ideological ties as well as through political ones. The Middle Ages, sometimes called the Dark Ages, were a troubled time for many nations and for many peoples. Yet through even the darkest times, the Christian nations had a saving and a comforting faith. The Christian Lord had become the shepherd of the western world, and the Christian people believed in the words of the psalm:

> "Goodness and love unfailing, these will follow me
> all the days of my life,
> And I shall dwell in the house of the Lord
> My whole life long."

Giotto's fresco *Joachim retires amongst the shepherds of his flock*

Boboli Garden, Florence: *Artichoke Fountain*

Stadium in Trieste, Italy

CHAPTER FIVE

Rinascimento: Age Of Discovery

Christopher Columbus was a giant of his time. He was taller than most men of the fifteenth century. He had red hair which turned white at an early age, a pale complexion which blushed to crimson at the least emotion, piercing grey eyes, and an indomitable dream. Born in 1451 in the town of Genoa, son of a wool weaver, Columbus dreamed of sailing westward across the Ocean Sea to reach the fabled golden lands of eastern Asia. He believed, but did not know for certain, that the earth was round, and that, by setting a steady course across untried seas, he would pass the point where west meets east, and set ashore in the empire of the great and legendary Kublai Khan, ruler of China. Driven by the power of his ambition, armed with the strength of his belief and the courage of his convictions, Columbus managed to persuade Isabela, Queen of Spain, to finance his westward voyage. In August of the year 1492, he embarked from Spain with a company of three ships and about a hundred men, on the journey which was to change the course of history.

From Spain, the three ships - the Nina, the Pinta, and the Santa Maria - made their way to the Canary Islands. From there, they set sail again on September 6, leaving the comfort of the known world for the watery enigma of the Atlantic, which they knew only as the Ocean Sea. On the ninth of September, they lost sight of land, and with only the compass and the faith of Columbus to guide them, they forged across a seemingly endless plane of undulating waters, out of sight of land, not knowing where the wind at their backs was driving them, or when, if ever, they would be able to return. For thirty days they faced the void, pressing ever forward with the wind blowing behind them, surrounded on all sides by the illimitable waste of the ocean, and the even more terrifying lack of knowledge about what lay in front of them.

In this day of technological wizardry, of two hour flights from Paris to New York, of super-computers monitoring every move of distant military maneuvers, of satellite probes with their video cameras recording images from space, it is hard to imagine the hugeness of the unknown into which Columbus launched his three ships. The first astronauts to reach the moon knew exactly where they were going, were in constant communication with men on earth, and knew, moreover, that the trip could be accomplished: after all, unmanned ships had reached the moon safely before and come back to the earth again. By contrast, Columbus and his men had no way of being sure that the Ocean Sea really had an end, and, even if it did, that it was possible to reach it. Although many educated men, Columbus among them, thought the earth was round, this supposition had never been proven and other theories competed with it in the hearts and minds of the people. Some were certain the earth was flat, like a pie plate, and travelling westward across the sea would only bring one to the earth's edge, where one would fall forever into a void. Others heard rumors that at a certain point far from land, the sea became hotter and hotter and eventually boiled furiously, killing those who ventured into it and even burning the wood of their ships. From the earliest days of civilization, unnerving stories have abounded about unknown realms of the sea; about strange creatures who live in the deep - mermaids and leviathans and sea monsters with appetites huge and hideous.

Into this unknown realm, Columbus sailed fearlessly, and it was only through his extraordinary courage, dedication and leadership that the three ships reached land on the other side of the sea. He wrote in his log that he would not sleep on the voyage, to keep a look-out for the land of which he had dreamed. The crew members remarked that he stood long hours on deck, staring into the night, "drunk with the stars." Convinced they were following

[88]

the hallucinations of a madman to their own perdition, his crew contemplated mutiny. The air grew hotter as the ships neared the West Indian Islands, and some of the men fretted over legends of boiling seas. The wind blew relentlessly behind them, and with each passing day it seemed less and less likely they would ever return home again. They glided noiselessly through pools of thick yellow seaweed, which the crew feared would mire the ships in tangled sticky webs. One evening, they thought they sighted land, only to have it vanish in the light of day. For reasons the crew could not understand, the compass appeared to alter its course with regards to the North Star. Thirty days and thirty nights they spent, totally at sea, following the course set by Columbus, whose faith in his vision never wavered. On October 12, just two days after the men had muttered of mutiny, land peered up from behind the horizon, and Columbus's long-cherished belief found its vindication.

To his dying day, Columbus never realized that the lands which he discovered on his four trips across the Ocean Sea were not in Asia at all, but two great continents, heretofore unimagined by European civilization. The Americas, as many people know, were named after another Italian navigator and map-maker, a Florentine called Amerigo Vespucci, who followed in the footsteps of Columbus. The first sea captain to land in North America was also an Italian, who, sailing for the British King Henry VII, became known as John Cabot. Cabot, born Giovanni Cabotto, landed in present day Canada. Like Columbus, he believed that the lands he discovered were actually part of Asia. On his second trip to North America, he sailed southward, hoping to reach the island of Japan. Needless to say, his hopes were in vain: instead of locating a rich oriental trade route, all he found was Massachusetts.

It is no mere coincidence that Columbus, Vespucci and Cabotto were all three Italians. By the late middle ages, several Italian city states, notably Venice and Genoa had become formidable sea powers. Venetian and Genoese merchants had established trade routes with cities of the Near East and used to sail routinely across the Mediterranean. Venice had even set up a mini-empire in the eastern Mediterranean, ruling over several small islands and a quarter of Constantinople. The Italians had learned to be at home on the water, and, because of their familiarity with sea-travel, they were the natural born leaders of the age of exploration and discovery.

In fact, during the century that Columbus discovered America, and during the centuries before it and after it, the Italians were, seemingly, the natural born leaders of just about everything. If Columbus was a giant of his age, he was born in an era of titans. In 1452, just one year after the birth of Columbus, Leonardo Da Vinci was born in Anchiano, a small town in Tuscany, northern Italy. Michelangelo was born some twenty three years later in Caprese, another town in Tuscany, and Raphael was born eight years after him in Urbino. The Medici family of Florence made a fortune in banking and used their money and influence to promote scholarship and the arts. In the same city, international diplomacy reached its pinnacle, and Machiavelli, the father of political science, wrote about political power. After a period of relative stagnation, Italy was creative again, rebuilding and beautifying her cities, establishing museums, universities and libraries, producing works of literature, art, science and philosophy. It was an age of tremendous cultural and personal achievement in Italy, a time of the discovery and rediscovery of aspects of the world and of human nature which had been unseen or neglected during the Middle Ages. This was the era known today as the Renaissance.

The term Renaissance was first used by French art historians of the eighteenth century to describe the revival of ancient architectural forms in sixteenth century Italian buildings. Later, the concept of Renaissance (French for "rebirth") was expanded to include the extraordinary flowering of art and literature which took place in northern Italy during the fifteenth and sixteenth centuries. Along with the flourishing of the arts, the Renaissance brought a new philosophy known as humanism, which celebrated the individual and glorified earthly, as opposed to religious experience. The people of the Renaissance were students of antiquity, who looked back fondly to the days of ancient Rome and Greece as times when human achievement was at its height. They consciously sought to emulate the Ancients in art, literature and philosophy, and they hoped to revive the days when Italy was the leader of the world. Because the people who made up this great artistic movement believed that they were bringing back to life the accomplishments of the past, the word Renaissance is indeed appropriate. However, because the rebirth of the days of antiquity began and reached its height in Italy, it would perhaps be more logical to use the Italian rather than the French word when we describe the achievements of the era. Henceforth, therefore, we shall say Rinascimento instead of Renaissance.

One of the most striking things which separates the Rinascimento from the times that came before it is the emphasis which was placed upon the individual. This emphasis becomes obvious when one thinks of the art of the Rinascimento. All of a sudden, works of art were no longer the anonymous contributions of a skilled artisan; they were the highly personal expressions of an individual artist, who signed his name to his work and who was recognized not simply as a craftsman, but as an inspired and almost divine human.

One of the reasons that artists of the Rinascimento achieved such a high level of skill and expression was, no doubt, because they were recognized as individuals. Personal expression was rewarded, and the best artists - those who won the many city-sponsored art competitions - were accorded fame, fortune and a special place in society. Artists were encouraged to realize their own deepest and most personal dreams; they were given license to follow their own instincts in the pursuit of beauty. It was this same kind of belief in the validity of personal dreams and ambitions which inspired Columbus to sail westward. Although most historians consider the artists of the Rinascimento and the explorers of the age of discovery as belonging to two separate movements which happened to take place at roughly the same time, the two are really inextricable. The Rinascimento was an age of discovery; some people explored the physical world, others explored the intellectual and artistic world of human experience. The discoveries of the Rinascimento formed the basis for our own modern world, both in our conception of the goals and ideals of human existence, and in our knowledge and understanding of the universe in which we live.

The Rinascimento began and blossomed in the city of Florence. Lying on the banks of the river Arno, Florence has always been renowned for its natural beauty and pleasant climate. The basic ideas of the Rinascimento started here: it was here that society as a whole, and the upper classes in particular, began to see themselves connected by a narrow ribbon of culture to the ancient glory of the Roman Empire. The Florentine nobles sought to strengthen that ribbon of culture, to use it to draw the achievements of the past into the present and to make themselves as great as their Roman forefathers, recreating the glory of ancient Rome.

Contemporary historians felt a renewing spirit enliven the city. A fourteenth century chronicler, Giovanni Villani, wrote "Our city of Florence, daughter and creation of Rome, is rising and destined to achieve great things." Nearly a century later, Marsilio Ficino, a humanist philosopher, wrote "It is undoubtedly a great age which has restored to light the liberal arts that had almost been destroyed: grammar, poetry, eloquence, painting, sculpture, architecture, music. And all that in Florence." Another contemporary historian, Leonardo Bruni, had no doubts about the supremacy of his city: "Florence harbors the greatest minds: whatever they undertake, they easily surpass all other men, whether they apply themselves to military or political affairs, to study or philosophy, or to merchandize." The Florentines saw themselves as leaders, and, even as they cherished the past, they looked to the future with sense of excitement and with the knowledge that they were at the helm of a great movement.

One of the conceptions that we have received from the writers and philosophers of that era is the idea that between the times of the Roman Empire and the Rinascimento there was a dark, sinister age, out of which "Culture" barely managed to escape alive. The people of the Rinascimento were so nostalgic for the glories and refinements of Rome, they believed that the achievements of their immediate predecessors were worthless, and could be ignored. Although it is certainly true that, until the Rinascimento, very few innovations or works of art, architecture or literature could rival those of the Romans, we would be foolish to think that the Middle or "Dark" Ages contributed nothing to the culture of the Rinascimento. Our modern historians are progressively uncovering more and more proof that the shadow which fell over civilization in the Middle Ages was not really all that dark. Although most people do not consider the Rinascimento as starting before the fifteenth

[92]

Pisa's famous Leaning Tower

Venice: the famous Clock Tower at the Basilica San Marco

Venetian palace

century, many of the founding ideas of the movement came from fourteenth century writers and painters. The thirteenth century, too, has been described by some historians as the "Greatest of Centuries." Many fundamental ideas sprang from medieval minds, and Florence in the fifteenth century would not have been the same without them.

One way in which the Italians of the fifteenth century differed from the Italians of Rome as well as from the Italians of today is that, from the fall of the Empire all the way until the nineteenth century, Italy was not a politically unified country. After the break-down of Roman rule with the simultaneous migration of Germanic tribes, Italy was fragmented once again into a collection of city states and foreign-governed territories. If there was any reason to call an era "dark" in Italy, it was because, suddenly, Italy was no longer able to dictate its own political destiny. Rome, and its surrounding territories, was ruled by Popes, many of whom were not exalted religious leaders, but were instead despotic princes intent only on enriching themselves. Many northern territories were presided over by German emperors, and many parts of Italy were included in short-lived empires administered by foreign powers who, to their credit, hoped to unify Europe in the way that only the Romans had ever been able to. The city states were often at war with one another, forming and breaking off alliances regularly, tearing the land asunder with battles and wars.

The Rinascimento brought no relief from the strife which ripped the land. Even in the most creative and highly cultured times, the Italian states struggled for territory, power and supremacy. They were bloody, dangerous years. The one thing which united all of the principalities of Italy was the consciousness that they shared the glorious past of the Roman Empire, and the belief that they were destined by their heritage to be great again. Just as the idea of the greatness of Rome inspired the ancient Romans, so the idea of the greatness of Italy inspired the Rinascimento Italian. While a Florentine might feel no particular political allegiance with a Milanese, both the people of Florence and those of Milan considered themselves the heirs of the ancient Romans, and considered the entire Italian peninsula to be their rightful domain.

Although Italy was beset by political difficulties, the Italian people could never be completely dominated by their troubles. During the Middle Ages, the Italians firmly established themselves as the richest, most commercially and economically sophisticated people in the western world. Italian states revived the art and custom of minting gold coins, which rapidly became international currency. The Florentine coin, the fiorino, or florin, was first minted in 1252 and was destined to be one of the foundations of her prosperity. We have already mentioned that the cities of Venice and Genoa were vigorously involved in trade and had substantial commercial interests throughout the Mediterranean. The Venetian and Genoese states had their own mints and made their own gold coin, called respectively the *ducato* and the *genoino*. These Italian coins, because the were made with pure gold, enjoyed the highest reputation of any in Europe.

The success of Italian merchants and traders brought so much money into Italy there eventually rose up a new class of merchants who dealt exclusively in money: the Italians became the foremost financiers of Europe. Banking houses leant money to kings of foreign countries who needed to pay their armies. Italian bankers set the international currency rates and travelled throughout Europe setting up Italian banks in foreign lands. The major financial street in London is still called Lombard Street, named after the Italians from the Lombard plain who settled there. It was the Italians of the Rinascimento who created many of the lasting institutions that banks and businesses use today, such as double entry bookkeeping and balance sheets.

The wealth of Italy, and particularly of Florence, during the late Middle Ages was another very significant factor in the rise of culture during the Rinascimento. Wealthy merchants wanted to do something with their money which would, on the one hand, bring magnificence to their city, and, on the other hand, afford glory to themselves. During the Middle Ages, affluent businessmen endowed churches. During the Rinascimento, they endowed artists. We mentioned earlier that one of the things which marked the difference between the Middle Ages and the Rinascimento was the emphasis placed on the artist as an individual. It was tremendously important that, by creating great works of art, the artists could receive not only fame and glory, but also money. The

Rinascimento could not possibly have fostered so much great art if it had not been for the wealthy people who paid for it, providing at least a part of the artist's impetus to create. By the time of Florence's greatest flowering, the Florentine people were no longer as rich as they had been during the Middle Ages, but the wealth concentrated in some individuals was what, more than anything, ensured Florence's greatness.

The fact that much of the magnificent art of the Rinascimento relied upon sponsorship means that we must count the eminent patrons of art among its great names. Foremost among these patrons in Florence was the Medici family, whose members, for generations, were the leaders and rulers of the city. Not only did the Medici direct the political fortunes of Florence, they were largely responsible for the city's pre-eminence in art. They sponsored competitions among artists, rewarding the winner by allowing him to carry out great works for the city. They fostered the talents of young artists, encouraging their work and bringing them into contact with a society of established masters. In the early days of the Rinascimento, they attracted the best artists into the city. Highly intelligent and diplomatic people themselves, the Medici stimulated creativity with more than simply money and prestige; they effectively nurtured the imaginative spirit of the entire city.

The Medici first appeared in Florence in the thirteenth century, when, through diverse trade and money-lending ventures, they amassed a huge fortune. Over the generations, various members of the family played an ever-increasing role in politics. The first major figure of the Medici dynasty was Cosimo, who, born in 1389, became known as *pater patriae:* father of his country. After being treacherously arrested and sent to exile from Florence for a year, Cosimo overcame his enemies and returned triumphantly to his city where he would rule as the effective lord for the rest of his life. Cosimo led Florence to victories in various battles and skirmishes against other states and practiced a diplomatic foreign policy which was designed to create a balance of power in the Italian peninsula. Greater than his external political victories, however, was what he accomplished for the culture of his city.

Cosimo had a tremendous fortune and an equally large

appreciation for harmonious architecture, magnificent paintings and expressive sculptures. He commissioned many of Florence's most spectacular buildings, employing and encouraging the greatest architects of the time, such as Brunelleschi and Alberti. He supported the work of such brilliant painters as Fra Angelico, Piero della Francesca and Masaccio. The superb sculptor, Donatello, whose statue of the nude David was a revolution in the art of human representation, was so grateful for Cosimo's patronage, he desired to be buried at the distinguished man's feet. In addition, Cosimo had the first modern library built for Florence, and he ordered the construction of a picturesquely decorated foundling hospital. Cosimo, who probably did more for the architecture of Florence than any other man, had a keen sense for the beauty of the buildings he helped to bring into existence. The chief attributes of these buildings, and, indeed of everything in Cosimo's life, was simplicity and grandeur. Alberti, who wrote about architectural theory, said "Just as deep notes on the zither or the lyre accompany the high and middle notes to produce a harmony which is joyful to the ears; so, too, there is a rhythm in other things, especially in buildings; for when they are ordered and placed in a proper way and in just proportions, they capture and ravish the eyes of those who study them." Looking at the buildings of Florence, one senses that Cosimo heard and felt this rhythm.

The next great Medici was Cosimo's grandson, Lorenzo, who was known as Lorenzo the Magnificent. Lorenzo typifies what we now call the Renaissance Man. He was highly cultured, well read and eloquent, with a deep and abiding appreciation for art, literature and music, as well as for the fine craft of living well and enjoying himself. Like his grandfather, Lorenzo was a political leader as well as a patron and sponsor of the arts. A poet in his own right, Lorenzo encouraged writers and philosophers, and his dinner table was frequented by the greatest creative minds of the day. Lorenzo promoted art for its own sake rather than for the purpose of embellishing the city; he was a believer in excellence for the sake of excellence. His whole life was lived in pursuit of beauty; artistic beauty, natural beauty, poetic beauty. Among the artists whose careers he further were Botticelli and Michelangelo. Lorenzo's court was always filled with genius. It was a meeting place of the minds; a nucleus of high culture in the most enlightened city of Europe.

Lorenzo and the people who surrounded him were members of a philosophical movement called humanism. This philosophy represented a renewed interest in secular life, and especially, in what it meant be a human living in the world. The humanists were interested in their own lives and their own relationships to society and to nature, and they were also fascinated by ancient philosophers, many of whom explored these relationships in their works. Humanists believed that people were capable of great things. For the humanists, man was heroic. Although they were far from being irreligious, they celebrated earthly over heavenly things. In their search for enlightenment, the humanists concentrated on the philosophical writings of the Ancients rather than on the stories of the Bible. Pagan writers, such as Cicero, Seneca and Plato came into fashion. Worldly experience and earthly perfection were seen as more legitimate goals than a paradise above.

One of the fathers of the humanist movement was the Italian poet Petrarca, who was born in Arezzo in 1304. Petrarca (also known as Petrarch) is best known for his sonnets; love poems written to an unattainable woman named Laura. The form of these poems was widely imitated throughout Europe and England, and the so-called Petrarchan sonnet shows up in many different literary traditions, particularly in English. Petrarca wrote the love poems which brought him fame in Italian, but the works of which he was most proud were composed in Latin. He was a tremendous classical scholar, so enamored of the writings of Virgil, Cicero, Livy and St. Augustine, he used to write them personal letters. In these letters, he addressed Cicero as his father and Virgil as his brother. In his writing, he sought to imitate the style and the vocabulary of his Latin forbearers. Recognized as an intellectual leader of his time, he helped to popularize the study of classical texts. Petrarca wrote almost constantly: when he was not writing poems and treatises, he wrote an extremely intimate journal of his personal life in which he explored his emotions and perceptions with an honesty and an intricacy which sounds strikingly modern. He also wrote movingly about the beauty of nature, and has been described as the first modern tourist, climbing mountains for no other purpose

[97]

than to enjoy the view and travelling simply to see how other parts of the world looked. Introspective and sensitive, Petrarca is sometimes considered the first modern man.

One of the foremost attributes of the modern man of the Rinascimento was that he was an individual with his own, unique personality and his own special talents and abilities. Although he was certainly religious, he was no longer strictly one of the sheep in Christ's flock. Artists and writers put a special emphasis on individual expression, not simply in their work, but in their lives and lifestyles as well. Petrarca shunned civilization for many years and lived by himself in the mountains, where he spent his days reading and writing. He cared little for the conventions of society but instead followed his own personal destiny, doing as he saw fit, heedless of those who considered him odd.

The artists of the Rinascimento were particularly flagrant in their disregard for social norms; in fact, during the Rinascimento, we have our first descriptions of the eccentric artist personality which today has become a stereotype. The painter Piero di Cosimo, whose mind was so occupied with his own lofty thoughts "those who conversed with him were frequently obliged to repeat all that they had said", is a good example of a man who lived only for his art. According to the Florentine painter Giorgio Vasari who wrote a volume about the artists of the Rinascimento, Piero's only food consisted of hard-boiled eggs, which he cooked along with his glue and his varnishes "to save the firing. He would not cook six or eight at a time, but a good fifty, and would eat them one by one from a basket in which he kept them." Botticelli is described as not caring how he dressed or whether or not his hair was combed. Then there is the story about the painter Uccello, who was so fascinated by his study of perspective he would sit up all night at his drawing table and refuse to go to bed. When his wife called him in to take his rest, he would exclaim "Oh what a sweet thing this perspective is." After his death, his wife complained that he loved perspective more than he loved her.

The art of the Rinascimento, like the poetry of Petrarch, looked back to the days of the Romans for inspiration, and, at the same time, paid close attention to nature. Artists studied ancient Roman and Greek statues and paintings in order to imitate the artistic styles of antiquity. Equally, if not more important than the study of ancient art, was the renewed and aggressive interest in the natural world. Artists observed ancient busts of Julius Caesar and statues of Greek gods, but they also attended human dissections at medical school. They were keenly aware of how bodies were put together, how they moved and which muscles animated each limb. Leonardo da Vinci, probably the greatest and most diversely talented human being of all time, numbers numerous anatomical studies among his works, including some, which, juxtaposing animal and human limbs, are among the first known studies of comparative anatomy.

Leonardo da Vinci, in fact, was so interested in anatomy, so keen to understand the exact mechanical workings and the precise details of the body, he himself dissected many human corpses. The sketches which he made of these dissections are so precise they have been compared to x-ray pictures. He did not limit his explorations to the workings of the human body, but performed equally exact examinations of leaves, flowers and animals. His art displays his utter, intimate understanding of the muscles and tendons beneath the skin, and the bones beneath the muscles, whether in his sketches of human faces, horses in movement, cats in repose, or birds in flight. A collection of these sketches, along with written descriptions of his observations and ideas, form the five thousand pages of his famous notebooks, which he kept throughout his life. In these notebooks he also made plans and drawings of various inventions, some of which are eerie premonitions of things to come. He drew models of machines of war; catapults and cannons, and he even hinted at the nefarious possibilities of submarine warfare. He described the workings of parachutes, and devised many possible models of human flying machines, including the precursor to the helicopter, as well as engines, automobiles, life-jackets and a multitude of labor-saving devices. He drew accurate aerial maps of cities and landscapes and made plans for perfect cities, with double tiers of roadways, the bottom for wagon and horse traffic, and the top reserved for pedestrians. Understanding the ways of human nature, he included every detail in his plans, even stating that spiral staircases should connect the top and the bottom layer of roads, saying these stairways should be round "because in the corners of square ones nuisances are apt to be committed."

Leonardo embodies the inventive, exploratory aspects of the Rinascimento. Although the ancient artistic traditions certainly influenced him, he was not a worshipper of the past. To the contrary, Leonardo believed that by attempting to follow tradition, artists lead themselves only into stagnation. In everything he did, Leonardo tried out new territory, attempting new ways of seeing the world, and new ways of representing it. His desire to do things in his own way is one of the reasons many of Leonardo's paintings did not survive to the modern day: he was always experimenting with new ingredients in his paints and his varnishes, and, unfortunately, many of these new ingredients could not stand the test of time. Those paintings that did survive are among the greatest in the world, and Leonardo was clearly one of the most gifted painters of his or any time. His portrait of a faintly smiling woman, known as the Mona Lisa, is the best known and most looked at painting in the world. It hangs in the Louvre Museum in Paris, and is one of that city's most important tourist attractions. Any given day of the year finds a crowd hovering about the famous portrait, which is protected by a sheet of glass and cordoned off in a corral of velvet rope to protect it from the over-curious.

Like many other famous artists of the Rinascimento, Leonardo began his career in Florence, but moved on to another city where his work reached its height. Leonardo was, by his own admission, not a tremendously well-read man. He did not know any Greek, and until late in life, he could not read Latin. Stifled by the emphasis which Lorenzo dei Medici and his followers placed upon ancient Rome and classical learning, Leonardo left to work for a new sponsor, Lodovico Sforza, ruler of Milan. Florence held the key to Rinascimento art; almost all of the great artists of the day either came from Florence or were trained there. The Rinascimento spread largely because sponsors from elsewhere imported Florentine artists to enrich and beautify their cities and their homes. As Florence's fortunes declined, there were fewer and fewer reasons for her great artists to stay in the city which taught them, and so they moved on to other cities; Milan, Venice, and Rome. The roots of the Rinascimento remained in Florence, but the movement

[100]

spread like a vine, taking root and blossoming in other cities throughout Italy.

In the late fifteenth and early sixteenth centuries, the popes who ruled Rome and its surrounding territories were anxious to recreate the past splendor of ancient Rome in their own day. Many believe that the Rinascimento reached its height in Rome, restoring it to its rightful position at the center of Western as well as Italian culture. From the Middle Ages onward, Rome had always been a religious mecca, full of holy relics, mysterious shrines and healing images, to which the faithful would flock seeking relief from worldly affliction or pardon for their sins. The city itself, however, was in decay and decline, its monuments scarred by the axes of time and of invading armies, and even dismantled by its own inhabitants. With the revival of interest in classical heritage, Rome became a mecca for artists and scholars as well; people who came to study the ruins of the city, searching for glimmers of its past greatness.

Partially as a result of this secular pilgrimage, partly because of the ambitions of the wealthy, powerful popes, Rome emerged from the ruins, restored, renewed and resplendent. Reigning popes and affluent noblemen brought in the greatest artists of their day to rebuild the city. Pope Nicolas V, known as the first humanist pope, established the Vatican Library which collected and preserved Latin and Greek literature and became the model for libraries in Florence and Milan. Pope Pius II, his successor, a writer of poems and plays himself, sponsored large numbers of paintings, buildings, tombs, statues and monuments, not to mention jeweled objects, decorative chalices and inventive seals. The popes of the Rinascimento were perhaps the most lavish patrons of art in history, each trying to outdo the last in his glorification of the city. Unfortunately, although in theory people of the Rinascimento had a reverence for the past, in practice they were more interested in their own creations. Many ancient Roman structures were dismantled so that their raw materials could be reused to build new monuments, palaces and churches.

Just about every great artist of the Rinascimento had a hand in the rebuilding of Rome. One of most famous men to bring his talents to the city was the legendary Michelangelo. Like Leonardo da

[101]

Vinci, Michelangelo belongs to a group of artists who have been universally and unequivocally recognized as creative geniuses. He has been called the greatest monumental painter of the Rinascimento and the most famous of all sculptors since the time of the Greeks. The son of a nobleman, Michelangelo took an apprenticeship in Florence and soon attracted the attention of Lorenzo dei Medici. Unlike Leonardo, Michelangelo found nothing oppressive about studying and imitating the works of antiquity, and, in pursuit of artistic perfection, he set about the task of equaling the greatest sculpture of classical Greece and Rome. He was successful enough that, during his early career, a statue of a faun which he fashioned was buried in a flower garden, where it was subsequently dug up and sold as an antique. When it was discovered that the faun was not actually an ancient artifact, Michelangelo was regarded all the more highly for his skill in reproducing the classical form so perfectly.

Sculpture was Michelangelo's best and favorite medium for ex pression. In his early twenties he made his first visit to Rome, where he was commissioned to create several statues, among them, one of his most famous works, a representation of the Virgin Mary holding the dead Christ upon her lap. This Pietà, made for a French cardinal, shows Mary a young and beautiful woman with face that contains such a mixture of quiet grace and emotion, many viewers have thought it almost impossible that a human hand could have chiselled it. Five years later, after returning to Florence, Michelangelo carved his most renowned statue, a huge marble figure of the Bible story David, which has become a symbol for the art of Florence.

Although he excelled at and preferred sculpture, Michelangelo was also responsible for one of the most ambitious and well executed set of paintings in the world, the frescoes which line the interior of the Sistine Chapel in Rome. The paintings were commissioned by Pope Julius II, who summoned Michelangelo from Florence and charged him to paint the chapel as he pleased, forcing him to use his creative vision to its fullest extent. Michelangelo rose to the challenge, covering the ceiling with events from the Book of Genesis, including, at the center of the ceiling, the famous scene in which God transmits the spark of life to the newly created Adam. The paintings took many years to complete, and Michelangelo, who had to work lying flat on his back for hours at a time on scaffolding high in the air, found the job onerous. Frustrated by the amount of time Michelangelo was taking, annoyed by the noises he made with his clattering tools, not to mention his loud moaning from the discomfort of his position, Pope Julius threatened to throw him off the scaffolding. Once the pope even climbed up it himself and hit Michelangelo with his cane in an endeavor to speed his painting along. Despite the hardships which Michelangelo endured, the Sistine Chapel is a masterpiece. The German writer Goëthe said "Unless you have seen the Sistine Chapel, you have no idea of what one man is capable of achieving."

Michelangelo and Leonardo da Vinci were by no means the only great artists who worked during the Rinascimento. Quite to the contrary, the list of artistic geniuses of the time is so long it would take pages just to enumerate them. From Raphael and Botticelli to Mantegna, Donatello and Masaccio, Italy produced a tremendous wealth of sculptors, painters and architects whose works have filled museums all over the world. During the Rinascimento, competition between artists fostered new ideas and new ways of seeing and creating. Painting, sculpture and architecture became subjects of serious study, both by those who strove to create and by their critics. Art was elevated from its lowly position in the Middle Ages to an almost divine height, where it was discussed and analyzed by the greatest and most influential minds of the day.

Although the Italians of the Rinascimento continued to worship ancient Rome, the creators of their time surpassed the ancients in skill and in design, not simply because they had more advanced technology, but because they had a more impelling personal philosophy. The humanist spirit animates the art of the Rinascimento, bringing to it a stronger current of emotion and a more powerful, wholly human message. The spirit of the Rinascimento gave strength to human virtues, making men strive to be heroic, whether by creating colossal statues like Michelangelo's David, or by sailing across the sea to discover a new world, like Columbus. The Rinascimento began in Florence and spread outward in ever-widening circles, until its ripples were felt in such distant cities as London and Moscow. It was a turning point in the history of western culture: the discoveries, rediscoveries and creations of the Italians ushered in a new era of human civilization, an era in which the individual was supreme.

CHAPTER SIX

Europe in the Rinascimento

Celebrations can be difficult to contain. When one person - or one group, or one country - catches hold of something new, of fresh dreams and invigorating ideas which give life new and unimagined dimension, other people are bound to seek that person out to share his excitement. That person too, exhilarated by his discoveries, goes forth to sing his news to the world. So it was with Italy and the Rinascimento. Songs of cultural rebirth spread northward and westward, out of Italy and into countries still slumbering in medieval dreams. From all over Europe, artists and lovers of art made pilgrimages to Rome, Venice and Florence. Writers and scholars eagerly studied the books of the new humanists and ancient Romans alike. Political and religious leaders listened carefully to Italian philosophers. Wealthy lords tried to recreate Italian courts and emulate Italian manners, clothing and customs. Italian artists and thinkers travelled forth, awakening other cultures with their humanist philosophy and harmonious works of art. The western world was ready for new ideas and Italy had them.

And so the Rinascimento took hold of Europe, and, later, of the British Isles. Humanism was probably the most significant and popular Italian export of the day. It was not long before all of the western countries had their own bands of humanists who shared the same concerns and interests as the humanists of Italy. These humanists, like their Italian leaders, sought enlightenment both from the masters of the ancient past and from the new geniuses of the Rinascimento. They were drawn into Italy, both to study contemporary art and ideas and to be in contact with the ancient Roman world which had left so many traces behind it.

Italy had many lures for foreigners, among them its splendid universities. From the Middle Ages onwards, Italy's universities were famous for teaching law and medicine. With the dawn of the Rinascimento, they were renowned for teaching science, math and philosophy as well. People from all over Europe came to Italy to further their educations: as many as ten thousand students would take courses in a single academic year at the university of Bologna alone. Even the crown princes of such countries as Sweden and Poland studied at Italian universities. Italy's reputation as a center for learning was certainly justified by the high caliber of her university professors, among them such illustrious men as Galileo Galilei who taught math and science at Padua.

Like Columbus, Galileo was an Italian who made discoveries which would forever alter the way the world perceived reality. He was born in Pisa in the year 1564, the son of a musician. Over the course of his life, he made three significant contributions to the world of science. First, he made dramatic improvements on the telescope, which was invented in a crude form in Holland around 1608. Galileo's telescope, which was thirty two times stronger than its Dutch predecessor, enabled him to study the skies. Thus Galileo became the first person to see the stars and the planets close up. He discovered the satellites of Jupiter (one of which he named after a student of his, Cosimo dei Medici II, grand duke of Tuscany) and the presence of sunspots. He was the first to observe that the Milky Way was a band of distant stars and that the surface of the moon was irregular rather than smooth. Most important, he amassed a body of evidence which definitively proved that the earth was not the center of the universe, but rather a planet which revolved around the sun. In addition to his work with the telescope, Galileo made inquiries into the laws of gravity and motion, and he informally stated the principles of these laws, which were later elaborated by and attributed to Newton. Thirdly, he established the logical and mathematical principles of scientific discovery. It was Galileo who laid the foundation for the modern experimental method which is still used today by scientists everywhere. Galileo can be considered the father of modern mechanics, experimental physics and the scientific method, as well as one of the most important pioneers in the field of astronomy.

With such men as Galileo teaching at the Italian universities, it is no wonder that the western world turned to Italy for its education. In fact, it is astounding how many famous inventors, scientists and mathematicians studied in Italy. Of course, those who came to study in the formal halls of Padua, Bologna, Salerno or Rome were but small portion of those who came to Italy in the Rinascimento. Others, particularly painters, sculptors and architects, came to Italy to learn from Italian masters in their field on a more informal basis. Still others came out of curiosity, both to see the country and to observe at first hand the glamour of Italian manners, social and court life. The people of Europe recognized Italy's leadership in science and culture. What is more, they recognized their historical debt to the ancient Italians who first brought them culture during the Roman Empire. Europeans, like Italians, looked back fondly to the days of antiquity when their civilization was centered in Rome. They embraced the Romans from Italy as their ancestors, and they were nostalgic for their ancient cultural unity with the Italian peninsula. In this way, the Rinascimento formed the third Italian Empire. The Roman Empire bound Europe together with military, political and monetary ties. The Christian Empire, emanating from the city of Rome, united the west with spiritual and ethical bonds. The Rinascimento Empire was a realm of progressive ideas, attitudes and cultural values.

The spread of humanist ideas was made easier and faster by the moveable type printing press, which was invented in Germany in the middle of the fifteenth century. Before the invention of the printing press, books had to be laboriously copied by hand and were, consequently, scarce and expensive. Students of literature or philosophy could rarely afford their own books and had to rely upon public and private libraries instead. Once the printing press was invented, however, books could be produced rapidly and inexpensively. Suddenly most anybody who wanted to could have a library, and there was such a high demand for books that printing houses sprang up all over Europe. In the beginning, most printing houses and most printers were German, but it was not long before Italy became the center of the printing industry.

Italy had many printing houses, the most famous and influential being the Aldine Press in Venice. The Aldine press was founded by the humanist scholar Aldus Manutius during the second half of the fifteenth century and it was operated by Manutius and his descendants for just over one hundred years, during which time it brought forth more than one thousand different editions. The chief goal of the Aldine press was to produce attractive and affordable editions of the Roman and Greek classics. Many of the most highly regarded classical works both in Greek and in Latin, were first printed by Manutius, who also published the works of Petrarca, Dante and many lesser Italian writers. The Aldine press is credited with manufacturing the first examples of italic style print and it pioneered in creating small, portable books which were the prototypes for our own modern pocket editions.

With the advent of printing presses came a tremendous surge in reading, both for scholarship and for pleasure. Printing houses in Italy published popular works in Italian as well as scholarly texts in Latin, and the reading public devoured them eagerly. Among the most widely read Italian authors were Dante, Petrarca and Boccaccio, who were well known not just in Italy, but throughout Europe and England. Of course, technically speaking, none of these three men belongs to the Rinascimento: all of them were dead by the end of the fourteenth century, but they exerted a tremendous influence on humanist thought. Perhaps even more important to the humanist movement were three books written during the Rinascimento by Castiglione, Machiavelli and Palladio.

Baldassare Castiglione was a writer and a diplomat born in 1478 who passed his life in the most cultivated courts of Italy. His treatise on manners *Il Cortegiano* translated into English as *The Courtier*, was one of the most widely read books in all of Europe. More than simply an etiquette manual, *Il Cortegiano* lays out the rules for the conduct of a gentleman in society, stressing not simply his outward conduct but also laying down guidelines for the philosophy of his life. Castiglione's book is composed of a series of conversations among the courtiers at the court of Urbino, where Castiglione spent six years. The speakers discuss the perfect

[108]

courtier, the perfect noble lady, the prince, and the relationships among them. Castiglione's writing embodies the most idealistic aspirations of the time.

Castiglione thought that people were good by nature, and he believed in their perfectibility through education. His perfect courtier is polite, refined and cultivated. He has read the classics and is familiar with the literature of the day; he can compose poetry in Greek and Latin; he can sing and play music; he is adept at sports and he is a graceful dancer. Although he is bound by duty to serve his prince, he does not let his duty over-ride his own moral sense: for "In dishonest matters we are not bound to serve anybody." On top of all of his other accomplishments the perfect courtier is a modest man who does not put himself forward unduly, and everything he does is with an air of grace and non-chalance. Everything that he says or does should "appear to be without effort and without almost any thought about it." Castiglione follows his own advice on this point by making light of his achievement in writing *Il Cortegiano*. In his introductory letter at the beginning of the book, he says that he wrote it "in a few days." Please bear in mind that the book is over three hundred and fifty pages long.

The Courtier describes what we know today as the Renaissance Man; a man who is well versed in all aspects of knowledge and society, from politics to music, to horsemanship and painting. Our concept of the Renaissance Man comes largely from Castiglione: for generations, *The Courtier* was the handbook of proper behavior for European gentlemen. Although the perfect society of which Castiglione writes did not exist either then or now, the desire to strive for it has been an important force in our civilization. Castiglione's writing challenges its reader to be as pleasant and useful as he can be, and it reinforces the traditional Christian virtues of chastity, charity and honesty. Although most people today have never heard of Castiglione, his influence on our own concepts of what it means to be a civilized and well-brought-up person are immeasurable.

Niccolo Machiavelli, also a diplomat, wrote quite a different book about the duties of the courtier and of the prince. *Il Principe*, or *The Prince*, was a short treatise on the philosophy of government, which Machiavelli wrote while in exile from Florence. This book, like *The Courtier*, found its way into libraries all over Europe and England and had, perhaps, an even more lasting impact. Machiavelli's name survives today in most European languages and in English because of the principles which he laid out in *The Prince*. The American Heritage Dictionary defines Machiavellianism as: "The political doctrine which denies the relevance of morality in political affairs and holds that craft and deceit are justified in pursuing political power: political opportunism."

Where Castiglione is optimistic and idealistic, Machiavelli is pessimistic and pragmatic. *The Prince* states that a ruler should use whatever means he has to remain in power, even if it means being cruel, lying, cheating or betraying one's friends. He says:

> Everybody knows how laudable it is in a prince to keep his faith and to be an honest man and not a trickster. Nevertheless, the experience of our times shows that the princes who have done great things are the ones who have taken little account of their promises and who have known how to addle the brains of men with craft. In the end they have conquered those who put their reliance on good faith.

> . . .A prudent ruler cannot and should not observe faith when such observance is to his disadvantage and the causes that made him give his promise have vanished. If men were all good, this advice would not be good, but since men are wicked and do not keep their promises to you, you likewise do not have to keep yours to them.

Machiavelli's cynical philosophy, like Castiglione's optimistic one, was known all over Europe. Ironically, however, Machiavelli himself does not seem personally to be as Machiavellian as *The Prince* counsels. Machiavelli's other works, which are not well known, show that he believed in the more traditional virtues of honesty and integrity over trickery and expediency. Moreover, Machiavelli himself was not particularly successful in maneuvering himself into positions of political prominence. Despite what he wrote in *The Prince*, he was a good citizen who remained staunchly loyal to the state of Florence, even when its rulers betrayed him.

Another important book of the Rinascimento - of a different type altogether - was Andreas Palladio's treatise on architecture *I Quattro Libri dell'Architettura*. Although Palladio's writing did not have as large an audience as that of Machiavelli and Castiglione, his book was, nonetheless, quite influential. Palladio was a stone mason who was discovered and educated by Trissino, a humanist scholar in Vicenza. Trissino himself was a devotee of ancient Roman architectural style, and he exposed the young Palladio to the writing of Vitruvius. Palladio, with a humanist education and Vitruvius as his guide, set about to recreate the glory of ancient architecture throughout northern Italy. He designed and built villas, palaces, churches and government buildings as well as town and country houses. At the end of twenty years of work, he wrote *I Quattro Libri* which was a summary of classical architectural styles divided into four books and illustrated with his own designs. *The Four Books of Architecture*, like *The Courtier* and *The Prince* became part of every educated man's library. During the Rinascimento, Palladio's influence was not greatly felt outside of Italy, but, during the eighteenth century, Palladio's book and his buildings inspired a revolution in architecture. The style of building that he popularized is known as Palladianism, and is found in great abundance in Italy and England as well as such countries as Germany, Russia and the United States.

Although the three books that we have discussed may seem to be quite different from one another, they do share several common threads which make them a part of the rich and peculiarly mixed Rinascimento tapestry. The first element that the three books share is the most important to the Rinascimento: they all acknowledge a debt to the classical past: Machiavelli uses the actions of Roman princes as examples; Castiglione insists that the courtier be able to read and write in Latin and that he be familiar with the great literature of ancient times; Palladio constantly refers to the principles laid out by Vitruvius, who he refers to as "my master and my guide." Secondly, all three authors are self-conscious in a way that was not possible before humanist thinking: all three are tremendously aware of the culture in which they operate, and they acknowledge not simply that they are a part of the culture, but that they are, in effect, creating it. Humanism gave individuals the

[111]

power of directing their own lives and of affecting society as a whole. Thus, Castiglione's writing asserts that each person can change his behavior and make a difference in the world, just as Machiavelli's states that a Prince can attain greater power by being aware of his own actions and of their effects. All three books reflect the Rinascimento desire not simply to live, but to make living an art - whether it be the art of gracefulness and gentlemanly behavior, the art of manipulation, or the art of constructing harmonious and beautiful buildings.

The spread of the Rinascimento outside of Italy was not uniform. Although the Rinascimento touched and affected practically every country which makes up our western civilization, some countries shared it more fully than others, and some fell under its influence earlier than their neighbors. Outside of Italy, the country that most benefitted from the Rinascimento was France, a country whose culture has owed a tremendous debt to her southern neighbor since the days of the Romans. Many of the most acclaimed buildings in France as well as many of the most highly cherished French traditions were actually borrowed from or influenced by Italians. During the Rinascimento, France learned more from Italy than did any other country. Fancy French cooking is an interpretation of the elaborate Italian dishes which Caterina dei Medici brought into France when she married King Henry II in 1533. Caterina, known to history as Catherine de Médicis, also built and decorated the Tuileries palace and garden in Paris where she used to give sumptuous feasts for the court. Other distinctive French structures, such as the fairy-tale castles that grace the Loire Valley, were built and designed by Italian architects and adorned in typical Italian Rinascimento style. The refined, polite and artistic French court was modelled after Italian courts; French writers read and admired their Italian counterparts, French connoisseurs collected Italian art: everywhere France tried to copy Italy.

One of the reasons that the Rinascimento had such an impact on France was that the kings of France were impressed by the achievements of the Italians and they wanted to share them. One might even say that the kings of France were jealous of Italy - which might help explain some of the political events of the era. Historically, Italy and France have had an intimate political relationship, complete with the bickering, jealousy and fighting that intimacy can bring. During the Rinascimento, of course, Italy was not yet politically unified. The country that we know today was divided into states, many of which were ruled by outsiders. The kings of France, indeed, conquered or held hereditary claim to several of the Italian states, and in their excursions into Italy, they had ample opportunity to view, savor and covet the fruits of the Rinascimento. In 1499, when King Louis XII invaded Milan, he fell in love with Leonardo's fresco *The Last Supper*, and could barely be dissuaded from cutting it off the wall and bringing it back to France with him.

It was Louis XII's successor, François I, who was the most responsible for the spread of the Rinascimento into France. He modelled his own court after the courts of such Rinascimento princes as Lorenzo dei Medici, surrounding himself with artists, poets and scholars. A humanist scholar himself, he strove to emulate the manners and occupations of the ideal Prince as defined by Castiglione. He encouraged humanist learning and gave money to endow the prestigious Collège de France, where teachers of Latin, Greek, Hebrew, medicine and mathematics were guaranteed academic freedom and liberated from the reactionary influence of Paris's medieval university, the Sorbonne. In addition to encouraging the artistic endeavors of his own countrymen, François I brought numerous Italians artists and craftsmen into France to build and decorate his palaces and country homes, as well as to enrich the intellectual atmosphere of his court. It was François I who brought about the marriage of Catherine de Médicis to Henry II, his son. François I also bought Leonardo Da Vinci's most famous portrait, The Mona Lisa, which, hanging in the Louvre Museum, now numbers among France's greatest artistic treasures. François I even persuaded Leonardo himself to spend the last years of his life in France, where he was installed in a palace and paid a handsome stipend. In addition to Leonardo, François also imported the brilliant but eccentric Florentine goldsmith and sculptor, Benvenuto Cellini, who created ornamental candlesticks and salt cellars which delighted the king. Finally François I tried, but failed, to persuade Michelangelo to come and live in France.

The French court and society developed a humanist spirit and free intellectual climate which rivalled that of Italy itself. In France, as in Italy, scholars and artists were granted the highest of social positions and were allowed a large amount of freedom both in the practice of their professions and in their personal lives. No such spirit of freedom reigned in Rinascimento Spain, which, newly united politically, imposed stringent and fanatical religious strictures on its subjects in an attempt to forge social unity. The Spanish Inquisition, which in 1492 was empowered by King Ferdinand and Queen Isabela to expel Jews and Moslems from Spain, also kept tight control on Catholics, who could be tried for heresy if they implicitly or explicitly challenged the doctrines of the church. Nevertheless, humanism spread into Spain, where it transformed the art, literature, customs and society of the country.

Spanish rulers, like their French counterparts, regarded Italian princes and their courts as models for their own. Queen Isabela, in particular, followed the example of the Italian monarchs by surrounding herself with scholars, artists and writers, and generously supporting the efforts of scientists and explorers, among them, as we have already mentioned, Christopher Columbus. Isabela's court was frequented by Italian humanists, and by Spaniards who hoped to revive the achievements of the classical age in Spain. Isabela's reputation as a patroness lured Italian artists and intellectuals into the country, where they found positions on the court or teaching at a university. Italian and Spanish humanist professors, who encouraged classical Latin and Greek learning, engendered new dimensions in contemporary Spanish writing and society. One of these professors, Antonio de Nebrija, who taught at Salamanca and Alcalá, devoted his life to "uprooting barbarity from Spain." He set about the task of raising the level of Latin knowledge and writing to a classical purity and he wrote the first Spanish grammar, which established a national standard language in Spain, modelled, to a great extent on Latin grammatical rules.

Spanish literature came into its own during the Rinascimento, due, in large measure, to the influence of Italian writing, which had long been read and appreciated throughout the Spanish realm. The writings of Dante and Petrarca were popular and widely disseminated, and, as the Rinascimento progressed, other Italian poets made their mark on Spain. Spanish poetry flourished during the sixteenth century when Spanish writers began to imitate the meters and rhythms of Italian poets. In the middle of the sixteenth century, a Spanish humanist translated *The Courtier* into his own language, and the book was an instant success.

The physical architecture as well as the philosophical and linguistic structure of the country also benefitted from an Italian influence. Italian sculptors and architects came to build palaces for Spanish kings and noblemen. Spanish painters and architects made trips to Italy to learn from the Italian masters. The greatest Spanish painters of the day received their training in Italy. El Greco, who is known as one of Spain's most talented painters, could claim to be just as Italian as he was Spanish. Born in Crete, El Greco was trained as an artist in Italy, working first under Titian in Venice and later moving on to Rome. At the age of thirty six, he left Italy and moved to Spain, probably in hopes of being employed by King Philip II, who was decorating his splendid classical style palace, the Escorial.

The Rinascimento also spread northwards into the lands which the Roman Empire was unable to penetrate; into modern day Germany, and Poland and Czechoslovakia, as well as into the Netherlands and Belgium. Germany, indeed, had become a part of the Italian-influenced world during the troubled Middle Ages, when kings from Germany tried to recreate for themselves the power and the glory of the Roman Empire. Rulers from German lands, whose powers extended from southern Germany across the Alps and into Italy itself, called themselves emperors of the Holy Roman Empire, which, now run by Germanic peoples, was able to subdue the wild areas north of the Alps which had eluded the Italian emperors of antiquity. Through the leadership of the Church, Latin learning had permeated northern culture, and, by the time of the Rinascimento, German universities had sprung up in towns throughout the land, and Virgil, Cicero and Julius Caesar were widely read and studied by the educated classes.

Because the German rulers had such strong ties with Italy and with Rome, news of the achievements of the artists and thinkers of the Rinascimento spread quickly across the Alps. Students from German lands flocked to the Italian universities, while Italian professors went north to teach in German institutions. Although

[115]

German culture never had the refinement and grace of the Italian Rinascimento, humanism certainly did spread through Germany, bringing with it that spirit of inquiry and free thought which would eventually lead to the creation of the Protestant religion.

In Germany, Italy was acknowledged as the center of artistic learning. The greatest German artist of the time was Albrecht Dürer, who believed that the Italians held the key to perfect artistic achievement. He made several trips to Italy, spending most of his time in Venice, where he studied mathematical formulas for drawing in perspective. Dürer's greatest works show clear traces of their Italian inspiration; many of his best drawings and wood-cuts are direct copies of Italian art. Although Dürer's work is quintessentially German, without the influence of Italy he would have been quite a different artist.

The north also produced some important thinkers, such as Desiderus Erasmus who was born during the second half of the fifteenth century in The Netherlands. Erasmus was a leader among humanist scholars of the time, who produced many brilliant original works of literature and satire as well as a tremendously influential Latin translation of the Greek New Testament. Most of Erasmus's writing was intended for an international audience, and therefore, most of it was written in Latin, which remained the international language. Erasmus spent most of his life outside of his own country, particularly in England, France and Italy. While in Italy, Erasmus collaborated with Aldus Manutius at the Aldine Press.

Men like Erasmus contributed to the international appeal of Italy: one of the reasons that so much brilliance came out of Italy was that practically every great mind of Europe eventually came to Italy itself and added his own discoveries to those of the Italians. At the time of the Rinascimento, the people of The Netherlands experienced their own flowering of art and intellect which was independent of Italy. Dutch painters, who were pioneers in oil painting, produced magnificent works of art from a different perspective than the great Italians. Some might even argue that the body of Dutch painting could rival that of Italy. However, the lure of Italy was such that even the greatest Dutch painters travelled southwards, where they were able to spread the knowledge of their techniques to the Italians. Thus, the greatest painters of Flanders, Jan van Eyck and Rogier van der Weyden came to Urbino and to Rome in the middle of the fifteenth century, contributing their own artistic visions, as well as several paintings, to the treasures of Italy.

The Rinascimento also came to England, but, largely because of internal political and religious difficulties, it came late. England during the fifteenth and early sixteenth century, was far, very far, from Italy, in philosophical as well as physical terms. When Michelangelo was painting the ceiling of the Sistine Chapel, the English were still constructing medieval Gothic cathedrals. During the same era that the French were creating their splendid chateaux on the Loire Valley, the English were building fortress-style hunting lodges in the woods, complete with crenelated walls and drafty bedrooms. During the fifteenth century, England was largely cut off from Italy. Some early English poets, such as Geoffrey Chaucer in the fourteenth century, did know Italy and Europe. Chaucer, who was strongly influenced by Italian writers such as Dante, Petrarca, and Boccaccio, is one of English literature's great early writers. English rulers, too, were not entirely free from Italian influences. Henry VIII himself, in the early days of his reign, pro mised to be a great Rinascimento prince. Like his contemporary François I, he had a humanist education, appreciated music, and read Latin. But the political climate of England was not ready for the advancements of humanism, and Henry VIII's reign was marked not by any great flowering of the arts and sciences but rather by religious schism and civil war.

England had to wait until the middle of the sixteenth century for the cultural benefits of the Rinascimento. When the young Queen Elizabeth I took the throne, she brought with her the ability to unite her country and to bring its culture out of a medieval slumber. Elizabeth, like the humanist kings of a generation before in France and Spain, was a great patron of the arts who encouraged the education and development of the writers, artists, doctors and diplomats of her country. Italy was still the leader in terms of culture and scholarship, and it was to Italy that England turned. Englishmen went to Italy as tourists, families saved and sacrificed to send their sons to Italy to complete their educations at the university of Padua, Bologna, or Rome. Knowledge of the culture and the manners of Italy was considered indispensable to young men who aspired to a career at court or in diplomacy. Queen Elizabeth encouraged young courtiers to spend time in Italy, sometimes even going so far as to subsidize their travels herself. Italian customs, manners and mannerisms, dress and language became the hottest fashion in London. Those who did not have the chance to travel could learn almost as much from reading Castiglione's *The Courtier*, which was very popular in English translation.

During the reign of Queen Elizabeth I, Italian humanist scholarship found its way to England, and the classics, in Latin as well as in English translation, enjoyed a surge of popularity. Although the English could never equal their Italian counterparts in art, they did produce some very fine classical scholars and philosophers, and, most importantly, some of the greatest literary geniuses of all time. Rinascimento England produced William Shakespeare, Ben Jonson, Edmund Spenser and Sir Thomas More, all of whom benefitted greatly from an association with Italy and with Italian and Latin literature. For generations, Shakespeare scholars have argued over whether or not Shakespeare actually travelled to Italy. An astounding proportion of his plays are set in Italian towns, some of which he describes with such accuracy and detail, one cannot help but believe that he knew them first hand. Others claim that Shakespeare never left England and that everything he knew of Italy was from the accounts of others or from what he read in books.

Whether Shakespeare ever saw Italy or not, it was clearly the land of his imagination. He was not a great scholar by the standards of his time, but he did know the classics. If he did not read them in the original, he read translations of Plutarch's *Lives of the Greeks and Romans*, and he was acquainted with the writings of Virgil and Seneca, and with the poetry of Petrarca and Dante. The plots for many of his plays were adapted from Plutarch, and a few were borrowed from Boccaccio. Although Shakespeare is a very English poet, his writing is informed by the culture of Italy and the enlightened, liberating philosophy of the humanists. If he did not visit Italy in his body, surely he visited it in his mind. Italy, and everything that Italian culture stood for, was the well-spring of his

[118]

creativity.

In fact, to Elizabethan England, and to Europe as a whole, Italy was the land of many dreams. Writers saw Italy as a place where exciting things happened and passionate people lived out violent lives, which might explain why Italy was the scene of so many plays. Young men of good families longed to travel to Italy to become sophisticated. Those who aspired to be doctors and lawyers saw Italy as the country where they could learn from the masters. Scholars and philosophers saw Italy as the land which produced ancient greats and modern thinkers such as Machiavelli and Petrarca, as well as the place where they could go to meet and converse with the greatest minds of their time. The Rinascimento did not simply come out of Italy, it remained intimately connected to it. Cultures advanced and became part of the modern world in an almost direct proportion to how much contact they had with Italy.

The progress of the Rinascimento did not mean, however, that all the countries which came into its realm adopted the culture and the values of Italy itself. Indeed, the most significant export of the Rinascimento was humanist philosophy, which encouraged individuals and, by extension, cultures, to develop their own separate personalities. Italy did not tell the world what to think, but it did show it how to think. Thus, a writer like Shakespeare was inspired by things Italian, but what he wrote was distinctly English. Italy's culture did continue to provide a model for other nations to copy. Things Italian retained a certain aura of superiority even after the other nations of Europe had created their own Rinascimento societies. In Elizabethan England, the Queen herself preferred to have an Italian secretary, and many members of her court insisted on Italian doctors and lawyers. Italian clothing and style was admired and imitated in France and in England. The lessons of Castiglione's *The Courtier* were memorized by everybody who wished to be thought of as a gentleman, whether he were in Rome, Paris, London or Madrid.

The Italians of the Rinascimento set into motion the forces which make up our modern world. Once again, Italy found itself the leader of a major empire, this one an empire of ideas, books, art, and images. The Rinascimento had a profound and italianizing

[119]

effect on all of the countries of western Europe. Northern and eastern countries, too, felt the forces of the Rinascimento, although to a lesser extent. The people of Poland and Sweden benefitted from having Italian-educated kings, and Italian architects were summoned by the wealthy from as far away as Moscow to help build and beautify palaces and government buildings. During the Rinascimento, Italy reaffirmed its place at the center of European civilization. It was the country to which people went to become educated. It was the land which produced the most highly regarded artists, writers and scientists of the century. It was the source of all that was glamorous, cultivated and refined.

Most of all, perhaps, Italy was the land of history. During the Rinascimento, Europeans discovered and embraced their Roman ancestors, and all of Europe looked back to Rome as its ancestral city. For Europe, the Rinascimento was a glorious reunion with the days of the past as well as a promise of progress: of new ideas, new freedom of expression, and new worlds. Italian culture was not a foreign culture, it was the source of all culture, a source from which Europe had been separated during the medieval years, and with which it was once again joined.

CHAPTER SEVEN

The Age of the Grand Tour

In the center of the fountain, Hercules shoulders the world, while on either side of him, stone mermen blow their horns. Beyond the fountain, the great house rises into the mist, its domes disappearing into morning air. In the garden, a grassy path leads down to the elegant shape of the Temple of the Four Winds, which stands at the edge of the wood. From the Temple of the Four Winds, one can see a round, domed mausoleum, encircled by tall columns, which commands the top of a hill. Throughout the garden, stone urns and statues lurk in the shrubbery; some of them date from the days of ancient Rome's glory, others were made by skillful hands during the Rinascimento. Inside the house, though we cannot see them from here, the long corridors are lined with ancient Roman and Greek busts and statues which stand in display on pedestals, altars and mosaic tables. The walls of the great house are painted with scenes of musicians hanging over balconies, as well as with representations from mythology: Apollo entertains the nine Muses with his lyre, the signs of the zodiac parade around the interior of the central cupola. In another room, a collection of Italian landscape paintings decorate the walls. The views from the windows of the house resemble, and even rival these idealized paintings.

Where is this place? Is it near Florence or outside of Rome? Perhaps it is in a suburb of Venice, where the mists waft in from the sea?

No, guess again. It is much farther north, not in Italy, nor even in France. This is Castle Howard, an eighteenth century mansion perched on the edge of the wild Yorkshire moors in England. The statues and the paintings were imported from Italy. The fountain was copied from an Italian original. The layout of the gardens was inspired by seventeenth and eighteenth century Italian landscape paintings by such men as Salvator Rosa and Claude Lorrain (who, despite the French name, did all of his important work in Italy and is considered an Italian artist.) The house, the temples and the mausoleum owe much of their form to the architectural principles delineated by the Roman architect, Vitruvius, and Palladio, his sixteenth century interpreter. The look and the feel of the buildings and gardens is Italian. If one were set down one morning in front of this fountain, one might never doubt that one was in Italy, were it not for the damp chill in the air.

Castle Howard is by no means the only mansion in England which could be mistaken for an Italian Rinascimento palazzo. England, along with the rest of Europe, has quite a large share of great houses that were conceived on an Italian plan. After the end of Italy's Rinascimento, the influence of Italian style continued to grow in England, where, from the middle of the seventeenth century onwards, wealth accumulated among the upper classes. As the English people got richer, they sought to express their higher standard of living with a higher standard of culture. Accordingly, they turned to the Italians as their teachers and their models. The eighteenth century upper class Englishmen wanted to live like sixteenth century upper class Italians. They wanted beautiful and ornate houses filled with paintings and sculptures. They were particularly interested in anything that came from the Romans, whether it was a marble bust of an emperor, a vase, or a temple to a pagan god. Like the Italians of the Rinascimento, the eighteenth century English saw themselves as the ultimate heirs of ancient Roman culture. It was only natural then, that their homes should be virtual copies of Rinascimento palazzi, whose owners saw themselves in exactly the same light.

The houses of rich Englishmen are not the only eighteenth and

[122]

nineteenth century buildings in Europe and England with Italian forefathers. In capital cities throughout the world, one can see many, many examples of Italianate architecture. Courthouses, post offices, government buildings, royal palaces and even train stations across Europe - any building that is supposed to inspire respect and awe in the citizen - tend to look like Roman monuments. Rome was everybody's model of a capital city, and so, as the European nations matured and began to feel secure in their own national identities, they built their capital cities on the Roman model. The spread of Italian style was partly due to the rising accessibility of books which laid out Roman architectural rules and principles. Vitruvius's *Ten Books of Architecture* was translated into many languages, reproduced and widely distributed across Europe. Even more popular was Andreas Palladio's *Four Books of Architecture*, which, as we mentioned in the last chapter, was required reading for anybody who wished to consider himself a cultured gentleman.

In the eighteenth century, however, there was one more requirement for being a cultured gentleman which was to encourage the spread of Italian style more than any book could ever do. The eighteenth century was a time when people from Europe, Scandinavia and especially England packed up a few necessities and headed out to see the world. It was an age of travel and of tourism, a time when (in the words of Dr. Samuel Johnson) an Englishman "who has not been to Italy is always conscious of an inferiority." During the Rinascimento, students and artists found their way to Italy to learn from the greatest minds of their time. In the eighteenth century, tourists flocked to Italy in droves, not to study with a particular professor or artist, but instead to see the splendors of Italian culture and to search through ancient ruins for a glimpse of the "grandeur that was Rome." Any well brought up upper class young Englishman was encouraged, and, indeed expected to finish off his education with a trip to Italy where exposure to the refinements of European culture was to make him "polished into a general and universal humanity." Travelling was deemed a necessity in the making of a gentleman, and the standard tour of France and Italy came to be known as the "Grand Tour." Returning home from his travels, which might last as long

[123]

as five years, the tourist could demonstrate (in the words of a contemporary poet) "How much a dunce, that has been sent to roam,/Excels a dunce that has been kept at home."

Starting in the middle of the seventeenth century, in fact, anybody who wanted to be a part of British high society had to have spent time abroad. Many of those who came back from extended stays in Italy or in France deplored the "solitary and inactive lives in the country" of the English gentry, and found their countrymen "rude, haughty and boorish." Those who had travelled abroad were eligible to join private and exclusive clubs. One of these, the Dilettanti Society which was founded in 1730, was open to gentlemen who had made the Tour (which they sometimes called by its Italian name the "giro"), and was formed to encourage the arts in England.

The Dilettanti were a group of amateur art collectors whose mission was to bring fine art into England. Nowadays the word "dilettante" is used pejoratively: a dilettante is somebody who (according to the dictionary) "takes up an art, activity, or subject merely for amusement, especially in a desultory or superficial way." In the eighteenth century, however, to be called a dilettante was a compliment. Dilettanti were lovers of art, science and music. They sometimes also referred to themselves as "virtuosi," meaning that they had a "special interest or knowledge in the arts and sciences." A dilettante or a virtuoso was, in essence, a man who, like Castiglione's Courtier, was well versed in the social as well as in the fine arts: he was a scholar and a gentleman. Perhaps in modern times we would consider a dilettante a frivolous person because he does not work for a living. In eighteenth century England, a gentleman, by definition, did not work to support himself. Dilettanti, then, were gentlemen who filled their considerable leisure time by learning about and fostering culture, much like the patrons of Rinascimento Italy. Dilettanti were eighteenth century Renaissance men.

Although the Dilettanti Society had a serious purpose - that of improving England's cultural climate - some other contemporary social clubs which required foreign travel of their members had more trivial goals. In the 1770's, for instance, some wealthy young men who had just returned from Italy, got together and formed

[124]

the Macaroni Club, which got its name from the members' favorite food. Macaronis, as they came to be known, were more interested in fashion and finery than they were in art or in culture. According to Horace Walpole, a distinguished man of letters who had himself spent time in Italy, the Macaroni Club consisted of "all of the travelled young men who wear long curls and spy glasses."

Macaronis were widely satirized by contemporary writers and caricaturists, who maintained that they carried "to utmost excess every description of dissipation, effeminacy of manners and modish style of dress." The Macaronis were chiefly distinguished by "an immense knot of hair behind, by a very small cocked hat, by an enormous walking stick with long tassels, and by a jacket, waistcoat and breeches of a very close cut." The fashion leader of the Macaronis, a Mr. Charles James Fox, used to appear in London wearing red shoes and blue-powdered hair. He even used to show up at the House of Commons wearing a hat with an immense feather in it. In addition to their exaggerated style of dress, Macaronis were fond of advertising their foreign experiences by speaking English words with an affected accent and peppering their conversation with Italian and French words and phrases.

Despite the ridicule that was heaped on the Macaronis, they did, for a few years, have a profound effect on British fashion. Everybody knew what a Macaroni was, and people who wanted to be fashionable copied the Macaroni style of dress. Even some of the clergy had their wigs combed like Macaronis, wore tight fitting clothes and began delivering sermons in affected accents "a la Macaroni." Shop windows in London were filled with caricatures of Macaronis engaged in various activities: riding horses, studying, going on parade. Numerous bawdy songs mocked Macaroni customs and habits. The fame of the Macaroni even crossed the Atlantic ocean, and a reference to Macaroni dress can be found in the American song "Yankee Doodle." Macaronis provided an exaggerated example of the possible negative effects of travelling abroad. Although most people believed that a tour through France and Italy formed the mind of the young man who took it, many people were also apprehensive that a young man, particularly if he were very young and spent several years abroad, might become overly attached to the more elaborate clothing and freer morals of the continent and return unfit for the more conservative and decorous English society.

To guard against the possibility that a young man sent abroad to learn about culture would only learn about stockings, hairdos and ladies of low repute, the parents of the Tourist often hired a tutor to accompany him. This tutor, who was frequently referred to as a bear-leader, was ideally a middle aged gentleman with a knowledge of foreign languages and a familiarity with the classics as well as an unimpeachable moral character: "a grave, respectable man of mature age." The tutor was supposed to be an instructor, a guide, an adviser and a friend to his charge. He was to make sure that the trip was truly instructive and not just a way for the young man to pass a few months or a few years as idly as he could. He was to see to it that his pupil learned to speak at least a little Italian and a little French, and he was also to keep him occupied in a study of classical Latin, as well as of history and of art. Furthermore, he was to "watch over the morals and religion of his pupil," which, far from home, were in danger of being corrupted. English parents, who belonged to the English Church, were particularly anxious that their children not, upon seeing the Pope and living in the company of so many Catholics on the continent, decide to change their religious affiliation. Parents were equally afraid that their sons might be entrapped by low women or greedy matchmakers and return to England with wholly unacceptable brides. There are many tales of a young man, far from the constraints of home, entering into an engagement with a woman of his choice, only to find that his parents disapproved of her and disallowed the marriage. It was far better for English parents to engage the services of a reliable and strict tutor, than to have to disengage their son from an unsuitable match.

Of course, the shortcomings of tutors were many. Although several very well known British writers served as travelling tutors, many bear-leaders were ill-equipped either to instruct their charges or to manage them. Some of the tutors were even wilder and more apt to get into trouble than the young men themselves, and very many did not know enough to provide real, useful information about all the places which they visited. The young men who made the Tour in order to finish their educations were usually seventeen or eighteen years old, although some were older and others much younger. At the age of eighteen, a wealthy young man who was accustomed to having his own way would be difficult for an older man, of an inferior social class, to control. As a result, particularly in the later days of the Tour, many of the young men who took the Tour learned more about gambling, playing cards and consorting with ladies than they did about the art of Michelangelo, the poetry of Petrarca or the size of the Caracalla Baths. Sometimes young men were sent on the Tour specifically because they were getting interested in women - sometimes because they were engaged in a flirtation with a woman whom their parents did not want them to marry. It is little wonder that far from home, where morals were looser and women more available, such a young man should find himself involved in a love affair, or worse, take up with a courtesan. Although British society disapproved of pre-marital affairs, if they were carried out discreetly or far from home they did not damage a man's reputation (they were ruination, however, for a lady). As Samuel Johnson said, "If a young man is wild, and must run after women and bad company, it is better that this should be done abroad."

Of course, not all travellers were restless young men barely kept in check by their bear-leaders. Many people who made the Tour were genuinely interested in the cities they visited. Once the fashion of travel was established, men and women of more mature years ventured out on the Tour, as well, both for pleasure and for edification. Although some people clearly went simply because it was fashionable and if they learned anything it was only despite themselves, many others were immeasurably enriched by their travels. The eighteenth century Englishman, we must remember, had a classical education. He read Virgil, Cicero and Horace in school and he was conversant in Latin. When he studied history, he learned the stories of Rome and the Roman Empire. He had read the works of Julius Caesar and he knew the names and dates of important Roman battles. Moreover, England during the eighteenth century liked to think that it was a reincarnation of the Roman Empire. The first few decades of the eighteenth century are even know as the "Augustan Age" after Augustus Caesar. A typical educated Englishman had spent many years studying the politics, literature and philosophy of Rome. A trip to Italy made his education come alive.

The Grand Tour was usually a carefully planned affair which followed a prescribed route, taking the traveller as directly as possible to the culturally important cities of Europe. Although the itinerary would vary somewhat according to the tastes of the Tourist and the political climate of the time, the Grand Tour was no Grand Tour at all if it did not include Italy. Italy was, essentially, the object of the Tour, but on the way there and back, most travellers gained at least an acquaintance of France, and some spent time in Germany and the Low Countries. Leaving England, the Tourist would usually take a boat from Dover, across the English channel to Calais, France. From Calais, the Tourist would go by coach to Paris, where he might spend several weeks or months. After a stay in Paris, the Tourist would head for Italy, either by boat from a southern port, or overland, through Switzerland and across the formidable Alps. A large portion of the Tourists went home as quickly as they could after having seen Italy. More ambitious travellers returned from their Italian stay with enough energy left to explore Austria, Germany and the Netherlands, hitting such cities as Vienna, Dresden, Berlin and Amsterdam.

Once in Italy, travellers tended to slow their pace somewhat, lingering for a time in Turin or Milan, before moving on to the more popular "must-see" cities of Florence, Venice, Rome and Naples. Venice and Florence, with their many beautiful sights and their gay social life, delighted the English Tourist, who usually spent several weeks or months in each city, going to museums and trying to learn how to speak Italian before moving on to Rome, the most important city of all. Rome, which abounded in ruins, statues and artifacts from the ancient past, fascinated the English traveller, who regarded it as the cradle of his civilization. In order to feel that he had really seen the city, the Tourist was expected to spend a minimum of six weeks in Rome, and to pass at least three hours a day sight seeing. After Rome, the last important city on the Tour was Naples, and nobody who got as far as Naples could pass up the opportunity to see the volcanic Mount Vesuvius. Late in the eighteenth century, the buried cities of Herculaneum and Pompei were discovered, and, with their unparalleled view of the world of antiquity, they became one of the greatest attractions of the Tour.

We have said that during the eighteenth century, travel was fashionable, but it might be more accurate to say that to have travelled was fashionable. There was certainly nothing particularly fashionable or glamorous about the act of travelling itself. To the contrary, travelling was difficult, slow, dirty, and dangerous. When one considers all that a traveller had to endure in order to get to Rome and back again in one piece, it is a wonder that anybody made the Tour at all. The tradition of the Tour was shaped by its difficulty: because travelling was such a major undertaking, the Grand Tour had a "once and for all" quality which encouraged Tourists to explore thoroughly the cities they visited.

Travelling in Europe during the seventeenth and eighteenth centuries was far more difficult than it had been during the Roman Empire when all of Europe was united under one political and monetary system and the Roman legions kept the roads passable and free from thieves. The first problem was the act of getting from one place to the next. The roads in Europe were notoriously bad, particularly in Germany and in parts of southern France, not just because they were poorly maintained, but also because in many places they were never designed for carriage traffic in the first place. Getting to the continent from Britain was no trivial matter in itself. One writer remarked that even the road leading from London to the port at Dover was the worst in all of England.

The passage across the Channel was not exactly a pleasure cruise either. Before the invention of the steamship, those wishing to traverse the Channel were at the mercy of the winds, which were by no means reliable. One eighteenth century Tourist wrote of waiting nine days in the port before the weather would permit him to cross. The trip itself usually took just over five hours, although it could take as many as fourteen. The Channel was frequently rough and notorious for causing sea-sickness. If that wasn't enough, if the tide happened to be low when the ship arrived at the harbor in Calais, passengers, with all of their luggage, would have to transfer to smaller open boats in order to get ashore. This operation could not have been a simple or a pleasant one during inclement weather.

Most Tourists travelled by coach once they got onto the continent. They could either hire private carriages or take a more economical stage coach to their destination. Carriage drivers in northern Italy capitalized on the Tourist trade by setting up an industry resembling modern package tours, in which the Tourist would pay the driver a fixed fee which included transportation from one city to the next, as well as accommodations along the road. This type of package was known as a *vettura*, and the system was called the *vetturino* system. Unless the *vetturino* was very dishonest (which was by no means unheard of) travelling by *vettura* was generally the cheapest and most satisfactory way for people to get around. An honest *vetturino* would bring his customers to the best inns, and the inn-keeper would be anxious to make sure that his inn was clean and safe, so that the *vetturino* would continue to bring in customers.

Of course, some Tourists preferred to travel in their own carriages, which they would either buy on the continent or bring over from England. The major disadvantage of having one's own carriage was that the poor quality of the roads caused much wear and tear on the vehicle. Moreover, the carriage would have to be specially constructed in order to get through the Alps and into Italy. The mountain passes were so narrow that carriages had to be taken apart and carried across in pieces and then reassembled on the other side. The travellers themselves were usually carried through the passes in sedan chairs on the shoulders of Swiss porters. Most English Tourists described crossing the Alps as a terrifying experience, which it no doubt was, particularly if made in winter when the steep paths were covered with snow and ice and exposed to occasional avalanches.

Many Tourists wrote of the dangers of travelling across the Alps, which was certainly the most dramatic part of the trip, but there were other dangers along the road as well. Thomas Grey, an English poet who made the Tour with Horace Walpole, gives a dramatic account of one evening in Switzerland when their party was attacked by a starving wolf, which eventually carried off and ate Walpole's spaniel. Wild animals were less of a problem along the more domesticated roads of France and Italy, but highway robbers (popularly known by their Italian name, *banditti*) were always something of a threat, both to travellers on the road and to those sleeping in inns. Guide books instructed Tourists to carry with them portable locks in order to be able to secure their rooms from the inside, and cautioned them always to carry fire arms. As one eighteenth century writer remarked "Double barrelled pistols are very well calculated for the defense of the traveller, particularly those that have both barrels above and do not require turning."

Not all of the inconveniences of travelling were dramatic and life-threatening, however. There were quite a few political difficulties, even in times of peace on the continent; difficulties which would not have existed sixteen hundred years earlier in the time of the Roman Empire. During the seventeenth and eighteenth centuries, Italy was not yet a unified nation. Each separate kingdom had its own currency, required passports and visas from those entering or leaving its borders, exacted duties on merchandise imported or exported, and most cities of Italy also insisted that travellers be in possession of a health certificate, stating that they were free of communicable diseases. If the traveller could not produce such a document, he might be put into quarantine for forty days - the word quarantine is derived from the Italian word for forty. Some travellers wrote that they were even required to produce health certificates for their dogs and horses before being allowed to go from one Italian city into another one. Once the traveller had his papers in order, he would have to submit to a lengthy inspection of his carriage and his baggage, both to insure that he wasn't carrying with him anything which was forbidden in the city he was to enter (every city had a different list of prohibited items), and so that the custom officials could charge him a tariff on whatever merchandise was taxable.

Although some customs officials were lax in their inspection of travellers and their belongings, others were known for their thoroughness in searching through a traveller's bags. In Pistoia, they looked for tobacco and would seize all of the baggage if they found over a pound of the forbidden substance. Officials at the gates of Rome were particularly minute in their examination of a traveller's books and papers, to make sure that no forbidden literature would enter the city. Many travellers found this meticulousness particularly annoying. As one remarked in 1741, "It was

[131]

impracticable for us to keep a journal in a country where our papers and books were so liable to be looked into by bigoted inquisitors." Much of this scrutiny could be avoided if the traveller had a letter of passage from somebody prominent, or was willing to cross a few palms with silver. Of course, figuring out how much to bribe somebody must have been difficult, too, since the currency was different everywhere. Modern travellers have a hard time remembering simple exchange rates which are standardized and posted in the window of every bank. How much more difficult it must have been in the eighteenth century when the rates were not posted and the money used in Florence was different from that in Venice, as well as different from that in Rome, Milan or Naples.

All of the annoyances of customs regulations were compounded by the fact that it was difficult to find a decent place to sleep while on the road. A Tourist who chose to travel on his own rather than with a vetturino had to find his own accommodations, and while he usually went to places that had been recommended to him by other Tourists, sometimes he was forced to stay in unknown places. Inns were notorious for being dirty, beds for being infested with vermin and inn-keepers for being dishonest. Not that there weren't many comfortable places to stay while travelling: many Tourists wrote of being pleasantly surprised by the comfort of their lodgings, but the majority of travellers wrote of having at least one unpleasant experience. Lodgings within a city were generally safer and better maintained than those beyond a city's gates, so it was important for travellers to plan their journey in such a way as to arrive at a city before nightfall. After dark, most cities locked their gates, not to admit anybody from without until the next morning.

With all of the inconvenience, danger, confusion, discomfort and bureaucratic red tape which making the Grand Tour entailed, it is little wonder that the British traveller, accustomed to a higher standard of comfort and respect, should have complained. But even though the journey was difficult, and even though most people who set off to see Rome knew what sort of troubles they would encounter, the British still flocked to Italy in droves. During the height of the Grand Tour, it was estimated that as many as forty thousand British subjects could be found on the continent at one time. It was not only the British who made this secular pilgrimage to Rome; they were joined in smaller numbers by Frenchmen, Germans, Dutch and Scandinavians, who, like the British, regarded Italy as the birthplace and the font of higher culture. The lure of Italy was so strong it overcame dangers and difficulties to draw foreigners over the Alps and into its mild, fertile climate. The tradition of the Grand Tour lasted nearly a hundred years, ending only with the French Revolution and the tremendous political and social changes that went along with it.

In other words, the Grand Tour was difficult, but it was worth it. Italy, her art, her culture, but most of all her image, exerted a tremendous influence on British thought and imagination - so much so that many English writers describe the land as though it were an earthly paradise. From the earliest days of England's Rinascimento until the present, Italy has been the land of inspiration for the British writer. When John Milton depicts the Garden of Eden in his famous *Paradise Lost*, it is an Italian garden like those he visited on his tour of Italy before he lost his sight. William Beckford, a notable Grand Tourist of the eighteenth century writes of entering Italy much as a religious man might write about going to heaven:

> . . . We proceeded over fertile mountains to Bolsano. It was here first that I noticed the rocks cut into terraces, thick set with melons and Indian Corn; fig trees and pomegranates hanging over garden walls, clustered with fruit. In the evening we perceived several further indications of approaching Italy. Myriads of fire-flies sparkled amongst the shrubs on the bank.. I traced the course of these exotic insects by their blue light, now rising to the summits of trees, now sinking to the ground. We had opportunities enough to remark their progress, since we travelled all night; such being my impatience to reach the promised land!

Italy was the promised land for the British traveller, not just because it was the final destination of the Tour, but because it represented the highest aspirations of the British people in art, architecture, literature, and even, at least through the memory of the Roman Empire, in politics. As we mentioned earlier, the achievements of the Italians in the Rinascimento did not truly reach England until the seventeenth century. When Britain finally did become aware of the Rinascimento, Italian art gained tremendous popularity among the upper classes, and Italy was seen as a vast museum filled with all the most wonderful treasures ever produced. The British were hungry for the refinements of an older and more artistic culture than their own. They were enraptured by Italian music, and they flocked to the opera, Italy's newest contribution to western culture. Grand Tourists spent thousands of hours going to museums in Italy, such as the Uffizzi Gallery in Florence, where they could see for themselves the greatest art in the world. They were entranced by Roman ruins and they were gratified by the warmer, more hospitable climate of the Mediterranean.

Not all of the pleasures of Italy were intellectual ones. Many people who spent time abroad managed to pass their days in a social whirl, going to party after party, staying up late at night and sleeping until noon. An undeniable part of Italy's appeal for the British was that in Italy they could enjoy themselves far more freely and expressively than they ever could at home. Most Italian cities had their own populations of British expatriates who were always eager to include Grand Tourists in their social plans, provided the Tourist could produce the proper letters of introduction from the right people back at home. During Carnival season, the atmosphere of Italian cities was particularly gay and festive. Venice was the supreme city for the Carnival, and during the season as many as thirty thousand visitors, from all over Europe and the Near East, made their way to the city. Venice, with its canals and magnificent Byzantine architecture, was impressive and exotic in itself. How much more dazzling it must have been to the British Tourist during Carnival, when the streets were filled with dancing, the canals with regattas, and the evenings with operas, comedies, masquerades and balls.

The one thing that the British generally failed to appreciate in Italy were the Italian people themselves. In fact, the British loved everything about Italy except the Italians: they seemed to feel that only they themselves were worthy heirs of the Roman legacy. One of the reasons that the Grand Tour was so important to the British was doubtless because of the image of the Roman Empire. Britain was in the process of building her own empire, and the idea of ancient Rome stirred British passions. Perhaps the Grand Tourist looked down on contemporary Italians because, in his imagination, the Italians failed to maintain the Empire, lost control of the world that they once ruled and had allowed their country to be overtaken, fragmented and dominated by foreigners. Eighteenth century British writings are full of the theme of the fall of the Roman Empire, inspired by the general poverty of the Italian people in contrast to the ancient splendor of Rome. One of the most famous works of English literature was composed precisely upon this theme. Edward Gibbon, an upper class English intellectual, went to Rome at the age of twenty seven. Sitting on the steps of the Capitol one October evening, his imagination was flooded with images of the vanished glories of Rome, and he was inspired to write his life's work, a tremendous history which was called *The Decline and Fall of the Roman Empire*.

The Decline and Fall was an immensely popular book, which, as Gibbon himself bragged, was to be found "on every table and on almost every toilet" in England. Even today the book is widely read, and until quite recently, Gibbon was considered one of the world's best authorities on Roman history. The book begins with the second century, and presents a continuous history of the Roman Empire until the fall of Constantinople in 1453. Although the title of the history emphasizes the ultimate end of the Roman Empire, it must not be imagined that it was simply the failure of the empire which caught the British imagination. The British were deeply interested in the Romans; in what they accomplished more than in what ways they failed. One of the attributes which the British admired in the ancient Romans was their ability to get things done. The eighteenth century was a time during which science and reason were revered, and so it is little wonder that the pragmatic Romans were the heroes of the day. The Italians of the eighteenth century were, by contrast, seen as people who were unable to get things done: people who were ruled by foreigners, who were not united and who had allowed power and wealth to pass them by, even while possessing some of the greatest creative and artistic minds of the day. Thus, to the eighteenth century mind, the

Italians were a fallen people. Unfortunately, through books such as Gibbon's *Decline and Fall*, the prejudices of the eighteenth century "Age of Reason" have found their way into modern thought without much examination, and there are still some people who think that Italy's cultural leadership was over when the last Roman emperor was deposed.

Of course, at the time of Gibbon's writing, Italy's influence on the shape of Europe's culture was in one of its high points, nowhere more than in England. Italian political and economic power may have fallen, but cultural power remained in Italian hands. If the British wanted to create an empire in the image of Rome, it was only logical that they should build their cities and their houses in the image of Italian cities and houses. Early in the seventeenth century, a British architect named Inigo Jones came back from Italy, bringing with him Palladio's books and Italian ideas. He was the first to introduce Palladio's architectural principles into England, and during the twenty nine years that he worked for British monarchs, he was constantly employed in creating as well as in restoring classical style buildings in England. The great Palladian architect of the next generation was Sir Christopher Wren, who was also inspired by the works of Jones, and who was in charge of designing and rebuilding London's churches after the great fire in 1666. It was Wren who planned London's St Paul's Cathedral, which bears more than a coincidental resemblance to an Italian monument.

It was because of the Grand Tour, when people returned from abroad, their heads full of the magnificence of the things that they saw, that the Italian influence really made itself felt in England. It was not just that architects began to copy Italian buildings in an English setting, collectors actually imported them - not great palaces, of course, which would be too difficult to transport, but statues (there are some from Hadrian's Villa in the grounds of Britain's Chiswick House), and stones (there are some from Leptis Magna set up at Virginia Water), and even at least one temple (the Temple of Minerva Medici, which stands in the park at Kedleston). If the Grand Tourists can be said to have brought anything of value to Italy, that thing would surely be money. In return, they got a great variety of treasures. Despite the difficulty and expense

[136]

of getting merchandise through customs, British Tourists were not shy about buying all manner of art and souvenirs from the Italians, who were relatively poor and eager to make deals. Tourists returned with many Italian paintings, statues and artifacts, some of which were valuable Roman and Rinascimento originals, some of which were worthless fakes. One rich lord came back from the Grand Tour with such a collection of objects, he had to pack them in eight hundred and eighty seven bags. Other Englishmen, notably the Dilettanti, spent their time in Italy gathering together objects with which to furnish their homes, and made systematic studies of the Italian buildings which most pleased them in order to be able to reproduce them at home. Italian art works adorned country and city houses throughout England, influencing the style and taste of native British arts and giving the English countryside an Italian feel.

Of course, Italian style buildings and imported ruins alone could not make the English countryside look like Italy - no, *that* required a gardener. Young men returning from the Tour would often remark on the natural beauty of the Italian landscape, saying that nature in Italy was kind, and that the untamed landscape was like a garden. Before the eighteenth century, British gardens were regular and formal, inspired by French and Dutch formal gardens, which, of course, were ultimately inspired by Italian and Roman formal gardens. During reign of George I in the eighteenth century, the British taste in landscape turned away from studied formality, and turned toward the gentle irregularity of contemporary gardens in Italy. The old formal gardens were done away with and the grounds of great houses were redesigned to look like Italian landscapes, complete with Roman ruins (either natural, imported or manufactured) and Roman temples. The redesigning of British gardens was called "improvement."

Of course, not everybody who made "improvements" on their gardens had actually been to Italy, but they knew what Italian landscapes looked like - or should have looked like - from the now popular landscape paintings of Claude Lorrain, Gaspard Poussin, and Salvator Rosa. English gardens were modelled after these pain tings, which gave a romantic and idealized image of what Italy looked like. Gardens which had been improved were called "picturesque" gardens, and the more picturesque a garden was, the more it was admired. The word picturesque comes from the Italian word *pittoresco* which means "in the manner of painters." A picturesque garden was a garden that had been so carefully arranged that it looked like the subject of a painting. Thus, instead of having landscape painting copy landscapes, we have landscapes copying paintings: life follows art. Travelling around their own country, the British would keep an eye out for naturally occurring "picturesque" Italian effects. In 1778, a guide to the Lakes District even went so far as to direct tourists to travel "from the delicate touches of Claude, verified on Coniston-lake, to the noble scenes of Poussin exhibited on Windermere-water, and from there to the stupendous romantic ideas of Salvator Rosa, realized on the lake of Derwent."

Because the highest ideal of an English garden was to look like an Italian painting, Roman ruins, statues and temples were a necessary ingredient. They were required to balance the composition of the natural picture, just as they might be required to harmonize or dramatize the scene of a painting. Of course, not all picturesque effects were pretty and gentle. The painter Salvator Rosa included jagged precipices and broken, dead trees in his landscapes, along with dramatically darkened skies and evidence of ruin, decay and natural disaster. English landscape architects were suitably impressed by the drama of Rosa, and one of the greatest garden designers of the day, William Kent, actually planted dead trees in Kensington gardens.

Because of the profound impact that the Grand Tour had upon its society, England was a cultural island no longer. The Grand Tour affected everything in English civilization, from clothing and manners to art, literature, and architecture, to the very lay of the land itself. People who had never been to Italy and had no aspirations of going could feel the Italian wind blowing through the countryside and changing the British way of life. Even Jane Austen, one of England's most insular novelists, who wrote all of her books about small groups of people in the country, could not help but discuss the changes that were occurring everywhere because of the Italian influence. Her characters frequently refer to the theories of the picturesque, sometimes with respect, other times to mock them. An important incident in one of her novels, *Mansfield Park*, has to do with improving a great English house and its garden. Britain was once again connected to Italy, her parent culture, and Italy once again brought its civilizing power across the British channel.

The age of the Grand Tour was a time when Italy's influence spread uniformly throughout Europe and England. The neoclassical, Palladian buildings which can be found in every European capital, from Sweden and Denmark to London, Poland, and Czechoslovakia are a testimony to the respect in which other countries held Italian architectural ideas. Italian music, particularly the opera, could be heard throughout the western world, and Italian art decorated great houses everywhere where people had taste and money. Although the seventeenth and eighteenth centuries were not the most productive times for Italian genius itself (except in the field of music), they were a time when the rest of Europe, and particularly Britain, learned how to transform their own worlds by following an Italian example. The Grand Tour, besides giving several generations of British gentlemen the opportunity to visit the land of their Roman ancestors, brought Italian culture directly back to England, where it took new root and blossomed. The British recognized Italy as the birthplace of their culture, and they sought to emulate Italian culture in all of its glory. Because of the Grand Tour and because of the universal appreciation of Italian style, we can walk through a garden on the edge of the Yorkshire moors today and imagine that we are just outside of Rome - on an unusually cloudy, damp day, of course.

Giuseppe Verdi, brilliant opera composer

Gioacchino Rossini, famous composer and gourmet

CHAPTER EIGHT

Musical Italy

Next time you listen to a piece of classical music or go to the opera, thank an Italian. Even if the music was not itself Italian, you can bet that the Italian contribution to what you heard was tremendous. While musicians from many countries have composed great music, if it weren't for Italians, the world of music would be immeasurably poorer. From the Middle Ages until the First World War, Italy was the major source of musical innovation and inspiration in all of Europe. Italian musicians gave us many thousands of individual compositions and brilliant composers, as well as whole new genres of music. The opera was invented and developed in Italy, as was the ballet. Italians gave us such composers as Vivaldi, Scarlatti, Verdi and Rossini. At some point in their careers, almost all of the great European composers and performers, particularly the Germans, went to Italy to study their art. Today, Italian is still the language of music: most of the directions written in a musical score are Italian words: *piano, forte, staccato, crescendo, andante, allegro,* and so on. The terms *bass, tenor, alto,* and *soprano* are derived from Latin words. The system of writing music on a five line stave was also developed in Italy. Even our most familiar classical musical instruments were invented or refined in Italy: the violin is Italian, as is the piano. Today, Italian performers, particularly Italian opera singers, are among the most popular and sought after musical talents in the world.

During the eighteenth century, at the time of the Grand Tour, one of the major attractions of Italy was its music. Tourists flocked to the opera houses in Venice, Rome and Florence. There, they sought out and lavishly praised their favorite Italian singers. Italy was regarded as a land of song, not just because of the organized musical performances which abounded, but because the common people of Italy, the *vetturini*, the peasants in the countryside, the women who did the washing, all seemed to have a song on their lips. Even today, the people of Italy seem more likely to express themselves musically than people of other countries. The singing gondoliers on the canals of Venice are little more than a tourist attraction these days, but travellers to Italy still come back with stories of bakers and garbage collectors singing arias from *La Bohème* into the morning air. Opera is a major part of Italian popular culture. American visitors to Italian opera houses are often amazed to see small children standing through entire performances of *Rigoletto* or *La Traviata*, and hanging on every note. Italians often know the great operas so well they boo if a singer misses a single musical phrase. Italy is now, and has been, for at least the last fourteen hundred years, a land of song.

Of course, the history of music on the Italian peninsula goes back further than the Middle Ages. In the days of the Roman Empire, music was also important to the people who inhabited Roman lands. Unfortunately, however, although we know that the Romans used music both for entertainment and for religious and military purposes, we do not know very much about Roman music: we know neither what it sounded like, nor much about Roman musical philosophy. Although many Roman paintings and frescoes depicting musicians and dancers have survived and references to music can be found in the works of the great Roman authors, there are no known examples of Roman musical treatises. However, music was definitely a part of Roman culture, and there are many reports of the popularity of various talented musicians, as well as accounts of musical productions and competitions. One of the well known eccentricities of the Emperor Nero was his belief that he was destined to become famous as a musician: he used to insist on giving public performances upon his lyre, which scandalized the decorous Roman people. The Romans invented or developed several trumpet-like brass instruments which were used by the army, and a few examples of these Roman instruments have been uncovered. Romans also made organs which were partially powered by water pressure and were apparently used as accompaniments to theatrical productions. A clay model of one of these organs was unearthed by archaeologists at Carthage, and an actual organ was discovered in the Roman town of Aquincum in Hungary. The Aquincum organ is still in working order, but there is no way of knowing what tunes it once played.

It seems likely that Romans music borrowed from the traditions of other ancient nations. As we mentioned earlier, the Etruscans seemed, like the present day Italians, to regard music as an essential part of life, and were known to employ the talents of pipe playing slaves to enliven their banquets, dances and other activities. However, despite the prevalence of music in the Etruscan culture, we know no more about Etruscan than we do about Roman music.

We are in a better position with regards to the ancient Greeks, however, who left behind them a body of musical philosophy as well as around a dozen fragments of ancient musical compositions. After Greece became a Roman province in 146 B.C., Greek musical theory entered the Roman world, and musical teaching of such philosophers as Plato, Aristotle, Pythagoras and Ptolemy became an integral part of a good Roman education. In fact, music in the days of the Roman Empire was considered to be an important science, and, accordingly was taught to Roman school children as one of the seven liberal arts. Along with geometry, arithmetic and astronomy, music was one of the four disciplines that formed the *quadrivium*. Romans learned that music was far more than just an interplay of beautiful sounds which could delight and entertain the ear: the laws of music were thought to be intimately connected with mathematics, human passions, the movement of the stars, and the order of the cosmos itself. The Romans believed, along with their Greek teachers, that music was also a moral force; that listening to the right kind of music - music that followed the mathematical laws of harmony and order - inspired respectful, orderly and civilized behavior. Listening to the wrong kind of music - dissonant, disorderly music that disobeyed musical laws - inspired rebellious and immoral behavior. At first glance, we might today think that these classical ideas about the power of music are without contemporary validity. However, when one considers that there have been several recent movements against rock songs with violent lyrics and raucous instrumental accompaniment, it becomes evident that these ancient beliefs about music's influence are not outdated.

As Roman power faded, Christian power grew, and along with it, grew the influence of Italian music which spread itself wherever Christianity was welcomed. Of course, the music that came out of the church was originally not Italian music at all. The earliest Christian services were accompanied by songs and hymns which, like Christianity, grew out of Jewish traditions. Jewish religious services relied heavily on singing, both by synagogue choruses and by worshippers. The essence of religious music, both in the Jewish and later in the Christian tradition, was that its purpose was to glorify God. The instrument which could most glorify God was the human voice. Accordingly, church choirs sang with little or no instrumental accompaniment - at one point, an early Pope even considered outlawing instruments altogether! The choruses were made up of people who were, for all practical purposes, professional singers. The Christians gained a reputation very early on for taking in and fostering abandoned children, many of whom were then trained by the church to be in the choir. The body of song which made up such a large part of the Christian service was carefully studied: it was very important to give God a melody which was worthy of him. Schools for singing called *scholae cantorum*, were formed to make sure that the music of the church was of the highest quality.

Christians songs continued to grow and develop. Since there was as yet no standard, recognized way to write melody so that somebody who had never heard it could sing it, the songs were passed along from teacher to student, changing a little bit with each successive generation. In the beginning of the seventh century, Gregory the Great, a monk from Rome, became Pope. He set about the job of standardizing the melodies that were used in the church liturgy. His achievement in this endeavor was so great that, by the ninth century, he was credited with having written every one of the songs himself. Although it is extremely unlikely that St.

Gregory actually wrote all the melodies used in the services (he was only pope for fourteen years and the body of song is tremendous), he did succeed in making the songs of the liturgy uniform throughout Christian lands. He assigned particular songs to particular times of the year, in an order which remained virtually unchanged until the sixteenth century, and he reorganized the *scholae cantorum*.

The entire body of song that came under Gregory's direction became known as Gregorian Chant. Gregorian chants make up one of the oldest bodies of song still in use anywhere. More than anything else, it was the melodies of the Gregorian chant that unified the Christian world. Many people who became Christians were not fluent in Latin, and yet they were able to appreciate the otherworldly beauty of the Christian service. Pagan peoples from Ireland to Germany to Russia were attracted to the sounds of Christianity long before they could understand the words. Gregorian chant was the spiritual voice of the church, a voice which could speak to people of all nationalities and backgrounds and which drew people to the church doors. Christianity seemed to recognize that music could speak directly to the soul; beautiful singing was always an integral part of Christianity's attraction.

Even after the work of St. Gregory, music was not written and the chants had to be memorized by students in the *schola cantorum*. Not surprisingly, it took a long time for novice singers to learn the entire liturgy and to know which melodies went with the psalms and hymns they sang. Generally, ten years of training were required to produce an ecclesiastical singer. Melodies were not entirely without notation; marks called *neumes* indicated when voices were to rise and fall, but they could not give a clear path to the melody itself, and were useless if the singer had never heard the tune. Because the melodies were not fixed in writing, a considerable amount of improvisation and development still took place in Christian music, which swelled with the voices of many diverse cultures. Many attempts were made to improve the *neumes* so that they could be read and understood by those who had never heard the melodies they expressed, but, until the eleventh century, music was a language without an established written system. It took another Italian, this one a monk from northern Tuscany, to create the musical score.

Guido d'Arezzo, as the monk was called, probably came from the town of Pomposa, but he was driven from the Benedictine monastery there because of jealousies which his musical innovations aroused. He settled in the town of Arezzo, and eventually was called to Rome by Pope John XIX. Guido d'Arezzo invented a four-line musical staff on which he placed rectangular symbols for notes, much as we do today. He drew the different lines of the staff in different colors and marked them with an alphabetical symbol for the notes which each line represented. He established the musical scale as having eight intervals, or notes, which he named from A to G. The eighth note of the scale was A again: as he said himself: "just as after a course of seven days we start again from the same beginning, so that on the first and the eighth days we always have the same name, so do we name the first and the eighth tones with the same letter, because we feel that in natural harmony they agree in one tone. On the side of the staff, he marked the line which represented the C and the one which represented the F. If the melody was a high one, the C would be marked above the F; if the melody was lower, the F would come above the C. These symbols can still be seen in sheets of modern music: they have evolved into the C and the F clefs which are at the beginnings of every printed line. Guido's staff is also still in use today, although now it has five, rather than four lines.

Guido's staff suddenly made it possible for singers to sight read tunes they had never heard before, and, using Guido's system of musical notation, ecclesiastical singers could be trained in as little as five months instead of ten years. Even more important than making it possible to teach more efficiently, Guido's notation opened up the field of musical creation in a way which had previously been closed. Now that tunes could actually be written down, composers had a tool that enabled them to create and immortalize their musical thoughts. Even more, now that music had a written language, composers could write music which was much more complicated than before: they could write music with different parts and voices, music with harmonies and interlocking melodies, music with depth, height, and texture.

Even those of us who are not musical, who have never studied music, never sung in a choir, never played the piano, are probably already familiar with another one of Guido d'Arezzo's inventions. Everybody has heard the scale sung to the seemingly meaningless words *do, re, mi, fa, sol, la, si, do,* but how many people know that those words actually mean something and that somebody wrote them? Believe it or not, back in the eleventh century, Guido d'Arezzo established those words as symbols for the musical scale. They are actually the first syllables from the melodic divisions of a then well known hymn from the Second Vespers of St. John the Baptist, *ut queant laxis.* Each syllable naturally falls on a successive note of the scale. The verse goes like this "**Ut** queant laxis **Re**sonare fibris **Mi**ra gestorum **Fa**muli tuorum **Sol**ve pulluti **La**bii reatum **S**ante **I**oannes." The first syllable, *ut,* has been changed to *do* in most countries, including Italy, England and the United States, and the seventh note, *si,* is from the abbreviation S.I. for *Sante Ioannes.*

After Guido d'Arezzo's innovations in musical notation and teaching, music began to develop at a more rapid rate. Gregorian chant, which also came to be known as plainsong remained the basis for Christian liturgy, but other, more complicated melodies requiring different members of the choir to sing different parts also formed a part of the service. Plainsong was, essentially, a single line of music, called monody: everybody who sang was singing the same notes. Newer, more sophisticated music no longer followed a single musical line. Different voices sang different things: the new music was polyphonic: "many sounded." Composition, which relied upon sophisticated musical theory, began to replace the older methods of improvisation. Musical composers could, for the first time, call their creations their own. The invention of precise musical notation had revolutionized the field of music.

The Church was the center for musical teaching and of musical study, but it was not the sole fountain of musical expression in the world. During the Middle Ages, in Italy and especially in France, wandering minstrels brought songs and stories to the people of small villages as well as to kings, queens, and popes. Folk songs have always existed in Western culture, and these songs formed the background of more formal musical composition. Sophisticated songs and dance tunes also came into being, especially during the later part of the Middle Ages. By the dawn of the Rinascimento, the noble peoples of Italy were used to being entertained with song and dance. While secular music in France was more formal and composed, the Italians were more spontaneous and expressive. Outside of the church, music was purely for enjoyment, and everybody in cultured society knew how to sing and dance.

It was during the Rinascimento that the world of music truly blossomed. In the early Rinascimento, Florence became the center for musical study. Musicians came to Italy from all over Europe to entertain Rinascimento princes and to teach other artists both their music and their musical theories. Outside of Italy, the two regions which produced the greatest musicians were France and Holland. Both French and Flemish composers migrated southward, drawn to the courts of such men as Lorenzo dei Medici and Federico da Montefeltro. Italy took the best of foreign talents and merged them with her own native musical genius. In Florence and Venice music became a necessary ingredient of a noble life. The ancient theories about music being intimately connected to the rhythms of the universe were revived, and music was studied everywhere in an attempt to get closer to universal truths. Secular music was not alone in profiting from the revitalizing energy of the Rinascimento: church music also surged ahead. Intricate polyphonic choral pieces could be heard in Rome, along with dramatically improved instrumental music for the organ. Competition among courts for the best musicians, and competition among musicians for the best jobs resulted in more and better music than had ever been heard before.

In fact, an appreciation of and a talent for music was considered one of the requirements for being a true gentleman. In *The Courtier*, Castiglione writes:

> You must not think I am pleased with the Courtier if he be not also a musician, and, besides his understanding and cunning upon the book, have a skill in like manner with sundry instruments.

Music was no longer a passive entertainment for the upper classes. Not only did the Rinascimento bring into being a whole new generation of professional musicians, it also created a population of amateurs who could sing and play. Because the Italian nobility had practical experience in music, they had a better understanding of and a deeper appreciation for the achievements of the professionals. As the Rinascimento spread through Europe, this sophisticated enjoyment of music spread as well, and all cultivated people attempted to nurture their musical talents, and, more particularly, the musical talents of their children. Music was once again an essential part of a good education, and the days of private music tutors for wealthy young nobles had begun. Secular schools for singing and playing instruments rose up alongside the ecclesiastical *scholae cantorum*, and, while the Church still usually got the best musicians and the best voices, the secular music industry was on the rise.

In 1501, another Italian was the first to print musical works from moveable type. Ottaviano de' Petrucci, who worked in Venice, published books of masses, songs, ballads and madrigals. For several decades he had a monopoly on music printing and in his lifetime he published sixty-one collections of music from his press houses in Venice and in the small town of Fossombrone where he was born. His publications included works from many of the foremost composers of both the fifteenth and the sixteenth centuries. After Petrucci's death, Italy remained the world's center of music printing, and Italian sheet music found its way to all parts of Europe and the New World. The dominance of the Italians in these early days of music printing probably accounts for the fact that all countries usually use Italian musical terms in their scores. Early in the seventeenth century, composers began to indicate the tempos of their music by placing an Italian adverb at the beginning of the score: *allegro* if the piece was to be played quickly, *largo*, or *adagio* if it was to be played slowly, and so on. When the sheet music was distributed to foreign countries, the Italian words, of course, remained in the score. Italian terms and expression marks soon became the accepted standard in the language of music, and have remained the standard up to the present day.

During the Rinascimento many new types of songs, dance tunes and instrumental pieces were conceived, many of them in Italy and under the patronage of a Rinascimento prince. Since poetry and song were considered to be intimately related, many

[149]

composers set the words of the great Italian poets to music. The poems of Petrarca, Ariosto and Tasso found a new popularity when they were sung as madrigals by accomplished choirs. The madrigal, which was invented in Italy, was essentially a song with two or more parts sung in harmony. Madrigals were popular in Italy and they soon made their influence felt in France, Spain, and Germany as well. Nowhere was the madrigal more popular than in England, where native musicians borrowed Italian tunes and replaced the sonnets of Petrarca with those of Shakespeare, to forge a native English madrigal tradition. It was not long before English madrigal societies sprung up in imitation of Italian societies, and soon the English were composing their own tunes as well.

The Rinascimento also gave us one of the greatest ecclesiastical composers ever known. Giovanni Pierluigi da Palestrina, who was born in the town of Palestrina outside of Rome, composed over one hundred and five masses and two hundred and fifty motets, along with a great number of madrigals and other secular songs. Writing in the nineteenth century, Giuseppe Verdi called him "the real king of sacred music, and the Eternal Father of Italian music." Palestrina is known for having brought the art of polyphonic music to its highest and most sublime point. He is also credited with having persuaded the Church not to ban polyphonic music from its services. During the Rinascimento, the Church was going through difficult periods of revision and reform. Church music had become more complex and worldly. In 1562, the Ecumenical Council of Trent banned the use of secular music in the church, and would have banned the use of polyphony as well if Palestrina had not stepped forward to defend it. "If men take such pains to compose beautiful music for profane songs," he said, "One should devote as much thought to sacred song, nay, even more than to mere worldly matters." The nineteenth century French composer, Charles Gounod described Palestrina's music this way:

> This severe ascetic music, calm and horizontal as the line of the ocean, monotonous by virtue of its serenity, anti-sensuous, and yet so intense in its contemplativeness that it verges sometimes on ecstasy.

During the Rinascimento and the century afterwards, which is known as the Baroque period, musicians and composers experimented with new forms of music as well as with new types of musical instruments, much as painters experimented with new subjects and new types of paints and glazes. This experimentation went on everywhere that was touched by the Rinascimento spirit, but nowhere more fruitfully than in Italy itself, where newer and better instruments were created every year. Two instruments invented by Italians which were tremendously influential in their day, are still the mainstay of classical music. The first invention was the violin, which appeared in northern Italy around the middle of the sixteenth century. Although nobody knows for certain who was the first to actually make a violin, the first examples come from the small northern Italians towns of Brescia and Cremona. Although there is still much debate as to which of the two schools is the oldest, the Brescia school, which produced larger violins with more power and a darker, stronger sound, probably came before the Cremona school.

Most people acknowledge, however, that the first true genius of violin making was Andrea Amati from Cremona. Amati began making violins around the year 1550. A true creative genius, Amati recognized that part of the appeal of the violin was physical beauty, and his violins were masterpieces of craftsmanship. Although the construction of a violin relies upon a scientific understanding of acoustics and proportion, Amati, like all great violin makers, had what amounted to an intuitive knowledge of what wood, what sizes and what shapes would make his violins sing. Amati was very careful about the materials from which he constructed his instruments. It is said that he used to go into the forests of South Tyrol, carrying with him a wooden mallet. When he saw a tree that he liked, he would strike it with the mallet. If the sound was pure, clear, and resonant, he would have the tree cut down and use it to make his instruments. Andrea Amati trained a whole school of violin makers, and Cremona soon surpassed Brescia to become the foremost violin making town in the world. Andrea's grandson Nicolò, who began as an apprentice to his grandfather before the age of fifteen, carried on the greatness of the Amati name, and eventually surpassed Andrea in his

[151]

artistry. The Amati name was well respected all over Europe, and the best musicians and performers actively sought out Amati violins.

Amati violins are still used and treasured today by violinists and collectors from all over the world, and the only instrument that surpasses an Amati violin in tone, quality, beauty and value is a violin made by Nicolò's star pupil, Antonio Stradivari. Born between the years 1644 and 1649, Stradivari, like Nicolò, began his career as an apprentice while he was still a teenager, and by the time of Nicolò Amati's death in 1684, Stradivari was the best and most famous violin maker in Cremona and in the world. Until his death in 1737, Stradivari made violins that were not only beautiful to look at but had a superior range of tone and expression, an unparalleled freedom of response and an extraordinary adaptability of volume. Violin experts are almost unanimous in pronouncing the Stradivari violin as the most perfect violin ever created. One of the most treasured attributes of a Stradivari violin is its capacity to adapt itself to its player. As one violin expert put it:

> Great violins don't change their tonal character, but a great Stradivari is extremely flexible. It almost seems to merge with the player's style. They form such a happy unity that it isn't always possible to keep separate the player and the violin sound; in every case they belong together. The sound has its own beauty, woodiness, brilliance, depth, power, and magic, and always the player's timbre, charm, and personality as well. If there were such a thing as an "ideal" violin sound, this is it.

Nobody knows exactly how many violins Stradivari made in his lifetime, but estimates range from just over six hundred to as many as three thousand. Stradivari probably made about one thousand violins, of which five hundred and fifty have survived to be played in the modern day. Today, many of our greatest concert violinists use Stradivari violins, which are just as sought after now as they ever were.

The piano, the second major instrument to come out of Italy, was invented by a Florentine named Bartolomeo Cristofori in the year 1709. Cristofori experimented with his creation, and by the year 1726 he had arrived at all of the essentials of modern piano action. The name piano is actually an abbreviated version of the original name *piano e forte* which, in Italian, means "soft and loud." Before the invention of the piano, the harpsichord was the major European keyboard instrument. The harpsichord had several drawbacks: it could not be played loudly enough to fill large concert halls or to compete with other instruments, and it was not able to express subtle nuances of sound because its volume could not be varied. The pianoforte was an improvement over the harpsichord because it did not have this limitation. The name pianoforte refers to the ability to produce gradations of volume depending on the force with which the keys are pressed.

Surprisingly, the piano was not an immediate success, especially not in Italy, where it was virtually ignored by the great Baroque composers. German musicians were much quicker to recognize the piano's potential, and the Italian invention was adopted and reproduced first by German organ builders and then, later, by English harpsichord makers. Eventually, the piano became one of the mainstays of classical music, and, perhaps even more significantly, a popular instrument which found its way into many thousands of households, even into homes which could not boast a musician. As Ralph Waldo Emerson said in his essay *Civilization:* "'Tis wonderful how soon a piano gets into a log hut on the frontier."

Along with the development and refinement of these new instruments went an explosion of interest in music and in public performances of it. Just as the Rinascimento brought painters new fame as creative geniuses, the Baroque (the period from 1600 until 1750) brought composers and performers heretofore unimagined popularity. Girolamo Frescobaldi, a composer and organist of the early baroque period is said to have drawn a crowd of almost thirty thousand to hear him play the organ at St. Peter's in Rome in 1637. Arcangelo Corelli, a brilliant violinist, received invitations to play in cities all over Italy and abroad. The orchestra was conceived, based upon the supremacy of the violin, which now replaced the human voice as the ultimate expressive instrument. The public concert made its first appearances. The ballet was born in Florence and soon exported to France and from there to Russia. Amateur music societies sprang up all over Europe and England.

In all this, Italy was the leader. Great keyboard composers, such as Domenico and Alessandro Scarlatti created sonatas which would inspire German composers such as Mozart and Beethoven. Antonio Vivaldi, a virtuoso violinist, wrote concertos - at least 450 of them - which became a standard of excellence during his own time, and which were the musical models used by J.S. Bach. Although Vivaldi's music was largely neglected after his death, the twentieth century revival of the works of Bach has brought Vivaldi back into the spotlight, and his compositions are widely heard and admired today. His collection of four concerti, *Le Quattro Stagioni* or the *Four Seasons*, is probably the piece of classical music most easily recognized by the average American. German born composers, such as Mozart, Handel and Haydn travelled to Italy in almost a religious pilgrimage, in pursuit of the Italian musical spirit. Even if one wants to argue that the greatest baroque composers were actually German, it is undeniable that German genius was inspired, challenged, and nurtured by Italy. As one early twentieth century writer put it "The classical tradition is nothing more nor less than the Italian tradition."

Of all the contributions that Italy made to the world of music, none is more spectacular and unique than the opera. A distinctively Italian art, opera, like ballet, was born in Rinascimento Florence and soon grew and spread throughout the western world. Opera was conceived of by a group of young Florentine musicians, poets and mathematicians called the *Camerata Fiorentina*, who hoped to recreate the kind of music that the ancient Greeks used in their tragedies. Of course, the *Camerata* (which included, among others, Vicenzo Galilei, Galileo's father) knew no more about ancient Greek music than we do, and so the style which they invented was uniquely their own. The first operas were written by Jacopo Peri, one of the members of the *Camerata*, just before sixteen hundred, and the first opera whose musical score has survived, called *Euridice*, was performed on October 6, 1600, which is frequently considered the birth date of opera. The earliest operas used stories from Greek mythology for their subjects, and were performed for private and exclusive audiences: *Euridice*, for example was put on in the Pitti Palace in Florence as part of the festivities surrounding the marriage of king Henry IV of France and Maria de' Medici. From the beginning, opera was thus associated with royalty and special social occasions.

Opera caught on almost immediately in Italy, and within twenty five years, opera was the entertainment of choice among the elegant people of Florence, Venice, Mantua, Naples and Rome. Although the opera originated in Florence, it was not long before Venice, which had a long tradition of gala festivals and spectacular carnivals became the world's operatic center. It was in Venice that the term opera, which is short for *opera in musica*, was coined. It was also Venice which put on the first public opera and it was in Venice that the first public opera house, the San Cassiano theater, was built in 1637. Venetian opera became known for its lavish and elaborate scenery and special effects, which frequently overshadowed the singers themselves. Venetian stage mechanics recreated earthquakes, battles, thunder and lightening; the singers wore magnificent flowing robes and costly jewels; live animals were brought onto the stage and flocks of doves were released into the theater. In a performance of an opera called *Berenice Vendicativa* held in Venice in 1680, the cast included four hundred people, over two hundred horses, two elephants, two lions, and an assortment of wild boar, deer, and bears. Venetian opera was tremendously successful and popular, both with the Venetians and with visitors to the city. It became a custom to give out unsold tickets to the city's gondoliers, who were known to be particularly vocal in their appreciation of the show - particularly of the female cast members.

Of course, it was not always possible to have female cast members: the Church of Rome, following the words of St. Paul ("Let your women keep silence in the churches"{I Corinthians 14:34}), forbade women to sing not only in church, but on the stage as well. Composers, however, have always written parts for high voices: indeed, Italian taste dictated that the soprano, the highest voice, was the most beautiful of all. Medieval church music focussed much attention on soprano boy choirs. The polyphonic music of the Rinascimento and Baroque periods, however, was too difficult for young boys to master. For a time, the soprano gap was filled with professionals from Spain who specialized in singing falsetto. Then, in the year sixteen hundred, another species of singer made its entrance onto the musical stage in Italy. The age of the castrato was born.

The castrati were men who had been castrated before puberty in order to retain their high voices. The castrato's voice, according to reports, had a special, unearthly, thrilling quality and many of the castrati apparently had almost unbelievable lung capacity and staying power, and could perform seemingly superhuman feats of vocal endurance. Although the Church officially disapproved of castration, and even prescribed the death penalty for the performance of it and excommunication for anybody who was an accomplice to the act, once a boy had been castrated, apparently the Church had few, if any, compunctions about employing his talents. During the height of the castrati's popularity, a good castrato could attain such fame and make such a huge fortune, a great many Italian parents who hoped to escape poverty had their sons castrated in the false belief that the operation would turn them into great singers. Some historians estimate that as many as four thousand boys a year went under the knife.

The best castrati, were, indeed, the most famous and admired performers in all of Europe. Although they never caught on in such countries as France, the Italians, the Spanish and especially the English were enraptured by their amazing voices. The castrati found a special place at the opera, where increasingly difficult music was written the better to showcase their talents. People swarmed to the opera to hear them, and, after a castrato would finish a particularly spectacular passage, cries of "*Eviva il coltello*" ("Long live the little knife") would ring through the air. Probably the most famous castrato was Carlo Broschi, who took the name of Farinelli. Farinelli gave performances all over Europe, stunning audiences with the superiority of his voice and the strength of his lungs. Farinelli's voice could outlast and overpower the trumpet of the best trumpeter of the day and it could execute difficult passages more nimbly than the violin. When Farinelli performed in London, the whole city was at his feet. "Farinelli was a revelation to me," wrote one Italian poet living in London. "For I realized that till then I had heard only a small part of what human song can achieve, whereas now I can conceive I have heard all there is to hear." The rapture into which Farinelli threw his audiences overcame even the noble English reserve: "One God, one Farinelli!" a Lady Bingley was heard to shout out in the opera house in London.

It is not surprising, with the castrato's popularity, that most of the female parts in the opera were not played by women. Women were not forbidden on the stage in every city, but female performers were generally disapproved of on moral grounds. Not that there were no female opera stars, because there were; it was just that because few singing jobs were open to them, a limited number of women were accomplished enough professional singers to take on the extremely challenging operatic roles. Besides, not all of the soprano parts were written for women in the first place. Since the soprano was considered the most valuable voice and since talented castrati were the rage, many early Italian operas had male leads written for soprano voices. Today we might think it strange and farcical to hear Hercules or Alexander the Great singing soprano, but apparently eighteenth century Italians did not think twice about it.

The emphasis placed on spectacle, both vocal and visual, detracted somewhat from the art of the opera itself. Opera singers were international stars in the true sense of the word, and they frequently felt that they could take liberties with the score of the opera if they did not feel it displayed their talents to advantage: the prima donna syndrome came into being at the very dawn of opera's history. Rivalries between stars were often hot, and reports of actual fist-fights between cast members (even on stage, during performances) were not uncommon. Opera was tremendously popular, but not everybody who came to the opera went to hear the music. In fact, the opera was frequently considered a good place to go simply to socialize, and many opera-goers couldn't even say which opera they were at. Some historians have commented that, given the atmosphere of the opera in its first century, it was surprising that so many great composers gravitated to the opera.

But great composers did come to the opera, and, by the middle of eighteenth century, opera had become the supreme showcase for the greatest musical talents in the world; not just the best perfor-

[157]

mers, but the best composers as well. Composers, like singers, gained personal fame, and were invited to the courts of kings, queens and nobles all over the world. Countries which had no indigenous opera imported composers, sometimes with entire Italian opera casts and production companies.

The first authentic operatic genius came early into the world. Claudio Monteverdi, who was born in Cremona in 1567 and served as *maestro di cappella* of the cathedrals in Cremona and in Venice, turned his talents towards the opera shortly after the form first appeared. His first work, *Orfeo*, performed in 1607 in Mantua, demonstrated for the first time the extraordinary capacity of opera to express and excite emotions. Monteverdi's operas are noted for their intensity and their poignancy. Contemporary reports tell of the audience being moved to tears by arias in *Orfeo* and *Arianna*, Monteverdi's second work. Although Monteverdi followed the tradition of writing about subjects from the classical past, he was the first truly to humanize his characters and to imbue them with passions and feelings with which the audience could identify.

The latter half of the seventeenth century brought the next great operatic composer in Alessandro Scarlatti, who wrote at least one hundred and fifteen operas. Born in Palermo in 1660, Scarlatti had his first opera performed in Rome in 1679. Queen Christina of Sweden enjoyed the opera so much, she became Scarlatti's patron, and over the ensuing four years, Scarlatti wrote all his music under Swedish protection. Later, he was commissioned by the theater of Naples, whose operatic tradition was beginning to rival that of Venice. Although Scarlatti was not known for being particularly innovative, he did establish the tradition of beginning the opera with an overture. More important was Scarlatti's influence on such later composers as Mozart, Schubert, Bach and Beethoven. Although these German composers were undeniably brilliant musical geniuses, they did, like most composers, turn to Italy for their inspiration.

One German composer who was tremendously influenced by Scarlatti's works was George Frideric Handel. Handel was born in Halle, Germany, where he showed early musical talent, and set out to become a professional musician. At the age of twenty one, the lure of the opera brought him to Italy, where he met Scarlatti and other Italian composers. During his five years in Italy, Handel wrote Italian style operas, which were so popular his fame spread throughout Italy and back to his native Germany. In 1711, he journeyed to London, where his Italian opera, *Rinaldo*, was the first opera to succeed in England. Handel stayed in London where he continued to write and produce his Italian style music, and it was not long before he was appointed one of the three directors of the Royal Academy of Music. The other two directors were both Italian. During his reign at the Royal Academy, Handel established the Italian opera in England, bringing over performers and operas from the continent, as well as continuing to compose his own works. Later in life he would gain extra money as an Italian teacher to wealthy British children.

The art of the opera continued to grow and develop, but not always in the best directions. One complaint that many people had with the opera was that it had become too grand and too affected. In response to these objections, the eighteenth century brought a new form of comic opera called *opera buffa*, which delighted audiences everywhere. The *opera buffa*, unlike *opera seria*, had ordinary people as its subject and a light, sparkling, piquant musical score. *Opera buffa* appealed to a broader audience than did *opera seria*, and merrier operas began to fill stages all across Europe. One measure of the *opera buffa*'s appeal is the reaction that it provoked. *Il Matrimonio Segreto* ("The Secret Marriage") an *opera buffa* written by Domenico Cimarosa in 1792, was first performed in Vienna for Emperor Leopold II of Austria. He liked it so much, he invited the composer and the entire cast to dinner. When they were done eating, he insisted that they return to the theater and repeat the entire work. A year later, *Il Matrimonio Segreto* went to Naples, where it was received with immense enthusiasm and, although the cast was never again obliged to execute it twice in one night, it did run one hundred and ten successive performances.

The *opera buffa* had an even more dramatic effect when it appeared in Paris. In fact, it started a war. Not a real war, of course, with guns and bayonets, but a war of words and sentiments which was known as the *Guerre des Bouffons*, ("The War of the Clowns"). The *Guerre des Bouffons* was basically an argument about which kind of opera was better, the native French opera, which had become extremely grand and stately, or the new, light and sparkling Italian opera which made its Paris appearance in 1752 with a work by Pergolesi called *La Serva Padrona* (*The Maid as Mistress*). The war was carried out in newspapers and pamphlets, and the argument became quite heated. Benjamin Franklin, who was in Paris during its height, remarked that the French were extraordinarily lucky people if the biggest thing they had to fight about was which kind of music they should listen to. Eventually, the *Guerre des Bouffons* caused the French opera to split into two separate theaters; the *Opéra*, which continued to put on grand and elegant works, and the *Opéra Comique*, which concentrated on lighter operas, following the style of the *opera buffa*.

By the nineteenth century, the opera was firmly established all over Europe, and many countries had developed their own operatic traditions and styles. Opera continued to enjoy tremendous success in Italy, and just about every city on the peninsula had its own opera house. The first great Italian composer of the nineteenth century was Gioacchino Rossini, who was born in Pesaro in 1792, and who began writing operas before his twentieth birthday. Rossini wrote several serious operas, but his real talent was in the *opera buffa*, in which he excelled in every way. Rossini is particularly known for writing operas which developed a rapport between the singers and the audience. His most famous opera is probably *Il Barbiere di Siviglia*, which he is said to have composed in just thirteen days. This opera was so successful, it firmly established Rossini as the most sought after composer of the day. Still a young man, he was courted by monarchs and princes, adored by the public and showered with gifts. He travelled all over Europe and continued to compose operas at a rapid pace. Stendhal, who met him in Paris, declared "The glory of the man is only limited by civilization itself, and he is not yet thirty two." Rossini's operas, to this day, embody the lively, human spirit of Italian opera. As Thomas Pynchon said in his novel *Gravity's Rainbow*, "The point is. . . a person feels *good* listening to Rossini. All you feel like listening to Beethoven is going out and invading Poland."

Rossini eventually settled in Paris, where his fame as a chef rivalled his fame as a composer. Rossini, from the beginning, was

[160]

interested in food - both in cooking it and in eating it. He is said to have described himself a "third rate pianist, but the world's prime gastronome." In Paris, he found himself surrounded by the most brilliant wits of French society, who gathered at his home every Saturday evening for good music, elegant conversation and splendid Italian food, cooked by Rossini himself. At the age of thirty seven, after having written thirty eight brilliant and well received operas, Rossini essentially stopped composing. He spent the rest of his life in France, where he remained at the center of Parisian social life, thanks to his talents as a cook and a conversationalist. To this day, French restaurants offer dishes on their menus prepared *à la Rossini*. Although many of these dishes are doubtless later inventions, at least a few of them derive from Rossini's original recipes.

Arguably the greatest Italian opera composer was Giuseppe Verdi, who was born in northern Italy in 1813. Verdi's opera came to embody the hopes, desires, and dreams of the Italian people themselves. The Italian people, it must be remembered, were still not a single, politically independent unit. Verdi's life coincided with the *Risorgimento,* the movement which would unite Italy and throw off the shackles of foreign domination. In need of a national hero, the Italian people rallied around Verdi, whose operas came to symbolize Italian patriotism. His operas themselves hinted at patriotic feeling, and inspired audiences with lusty choruses, evocative melodies and strongly dramatic situations. Verdi wrote operas from the time he was twenty five until he reached the age of eighty. Among his most popular works are *Rigoletto, Il Trovatore, La Traviata,* and *Aïda.* Verdi's works make up a large part of any modern opera company's repertory, and are among the most popular operas of all time.

Although today the opera belongs to the world, its roots and its spirit remain in Italy. Great operatic composers and singers have come from every continent and every corner of the world, from Japan to South America, North America, Australia and Europe, but Italy is still the mecca of opera. Indeed, it is astounding, given the international character of today's opera, how many of our greatest singers are still from Italy. Enrico Caruso, who died in 1921, could very well be the most admired operatic tenor of all time. Born in Naples, Caruso achieved fame in roles from Puccini operas. He had a strong, easy, intensely appealing voice which was unusually rich and had a remarkable range of expression. Caruso performed outside of Italy, in Paris, London and New York, where he drew tremendous audiences and his name became legendary. Today, the most admired tenor in opera is Luciano Pavorotti, whose voice has frequently been compared to Caruso's. Non-Italian operatic geniuses abound, of course, but it would be hard to imagine an opera singer who did not feel a special bond to Italy.

Indeed, it would be hard to imagine any music lover who did not feel drawn to Italy. Although it is impossible to describe objectively why it is that Italian music is so powerful, many students of music will claim that Italian music and Italian music alone truly expresses the deepest and the best of human emotions. Italian music is direct and passionate, they will say. While German music may be more technically perfect, or grander, or objectively "better", Italian music speaks the language of the soul. Human beings are not perfect and perfection does not stir the heart. Italy is a musical land because its people express their emotions openly, enjoy life without guilt, and allow their creativity free rein. Historically, the world of western music owes a great deal to Italy. In spirit, perhaps, we owe Italy a great deal more. Italian music has enriched lives which are unconnected to the world of music. Like the Gregorian chant, which drew thousands of converts to the church doors during the Middle Ages, Italian music carries people towards the spirit of humanity. If music truly is a moral force, as the ancient Romans believed, then listening to Verdi or Vivaldi or Rossini must bring us closer to being the best that we can be.

CHAPTER NINE

Italian America

Where is Italian America? Is it in those parts of our major cities known as "Little Italy", where we can buy Italian newspapers and freshly baked pastries that remind us of mornings in Rome? Is it within the walls of New York's Metropolitan Opera House, where Italian voices sing dramas with Italian words, to melodies composed by Italian maestros? Is it inside the rooms of Italian American organizations, or in classrooms where American students memorize quotations from Dante, or in secluded studios where artists chisel sculptures out of marble blocks? If we look for Italian America, we must look everywhere, because Italian America is not just in the Italian sections of town. Indeed, Italian influence in America is so pervasive and widespread, we can find traces of it in every aspect of our society. Not only does America count twenty five million people with Italian roots among her citizens, but the very structure of American society and the ideas and ideals upon which our nation was founded grew out of Italian thought. It has often been said that America is the new Rome: a tremendous melting pot of different and diverse cultures, and the newest leader of Western civilization. Italy and the Italians have contributed many different ingredients to this melting pot of culture. Some of these ingredients have retained a specifically Italian flavor, while others are so well integrated into the American consciousness they are not recognized as having an Italian origin. Every

[163]

aspect of American life has been influenced by Italy, from the food we eat, to the laws we follow, to the performers who entertain us, to the scientists and inventors who make our world more convenient and accessible. When we set out to find Italian America, we must look beyond "Little Italy." Italian America is everywhere.

The relationship between Italy and America has a long history. America, after all, was discovered by an Italian, named for an Italian and explored by Italians. Columbus, Vespucci and Cabot were only a few of the Italians who took a major part in the establishment of the New World. Other early Italian explorers also helped to put the outlines of America on the map. In recent years, Italian Americans have fought successfully for the public recognition of neglected Italian explorers such as Giovanni da Verrazzano, a nobleman from Tuscany who sailed for the French King François I. Verrazzano, whose ship reached the New World in 1524, first sighted land off the coast of present day North Carolina, and turning northward, explored the coastline all the way up to Maine. His detailed accounts of the unspoiled and fertile lands that he saw hint at the beauty and potential that the young America held for Europe.

Although Cabot reached the coast of Maine before him, Verrazzano was the first European to describe the sights of present day North America, which he called Francesca, in honor of the king. Among his other accomplishments, Verrazzano is credited with having discovered New York Harbor, which was peopled by friendly Indians, and with having bestowed the name Rhode Island on the land which would later become our modern day state. Verrazzano, in fact, gave Italian names to many landmarks, although few of his names have survived. Cape Cod in Massachusetts, for instance, was called Cape Pallavicini, in honor of an Italian general who fought in King François's army. Over the course of four years, Verrazzano made three trips to America. On his last trip, he met a gruesome end. Exploring the Caribbean Islands, he made the mistake of assuming that the Caribbean Indians were as gentle and friendly as those he encountered in New York Harbor. He waded ashore to meet a group of them, where he was ambushed, killed, and then roasted and eaten while his horrified crew looked on.

The years during which America was first colonized were not good ones for the Italian states, and, perhaps because of this, no Italian colonies were established in the New World, and relatively few Italians came to America. However, this is not to say that Italians did not play a significant part in civilizing America. French, Portuguese, Spanish and English colonies all contained an unspecified number of Italian colonists who came to America in search of new opportunities. English colonists eager to produce silk in the new world, brought mulberry trees, silk worms and skilled workers from Italy to colonies in Georgia and Virginia. Venetian glassblowers also found themselves in demand among the colonies. Christian missionaries from Italy joined forces with missionaries from Spain and Portugal to spread the gospel to the south and west. Notable among these missionaries were Marco da Nizza, who was the first to lead expeditions into Nebraska and Arizona, and Francesco Chino, who built more than thirty churches and missions in California, and also wrote about astronomical phenomena.

Most important among early Italian American explorers, however, was Enrico Tonti, who undertook expeditions for the French flag, and is credited as the founder of the state of Illinois as well as, according to some, the state of Arkansas. Tonti, whose father Lorenzo invented and implemented the world's first life insurance system (a system which, by the way, is still called a tontine in his honor), was born south of Rome in 1647, and subsequently moved to France with his parents. After serving in the French military, he was sent on to America as second in command to the famous French explorer Robert La Salle. Along with La Salle, Tonti staked out the Louisiana territory, which would later become the Louisiana Purchase, an extremely important piece of the American landscape. Tonti spent several winters on the cold northern shores of the Great Lakes in the service of France. His dream, not surprisingly, was to establish French territory further south, throughout the fertile mid-west, and to shift France's colonizing efforts away from Canada and the icy north. Although Tonti was largely unsuccessful in this endeavor, he did significantly expand the French empire, and was instrumental in the founding of the French city of New Orleans. His brother, Alfonso, was the founder of the city of Detroit.

Enrico Tonti endured tremendous hardships in the American wilderness. At times the weather was extremely inhospitable. The woods were peopled with warring Indian tribes. To make matters worse, food was sometimes in short supply, and the men under Tonti's command were more than once on the brink of mutiny. One time, on what seemed to be a hopeless mission, they did desert him while he was out checking a fortification along the Mississippi river. They stole all the provisions, destroyed the fort, and left him only the message *Nous sommes tous sauvages*, ("We are all savages") carved into a plank on the side of a ship they were building. Tonti's physical endurance was all the more astonishing when one considers that he was missing his right hand. The hand was blown off by a grenade during the French wars against Spain, and thereafter, his right arm ended in a brass hook. Robert La Salle was initially skeptical about having a one handed man as his second in command, but Tonti's fortitude and unwavering loyalty soon dispelled his doubts. The Indians were in awe of Tonti, who seemed to them to have something of the supernatural about him. They called him "Iron Hand."

Although many Italian explorers and navigators took part in charting the physical territory of the New World, the Italian influence was even greater in mapping out the philosophy of the emerging American nation. The foundation of America took place, it must be remembered, during the height of the eighteenth century, at a time when Italian influence in English culture was reaching its zenith. The framers of the American constitution came from the same social classes as those Englishmen who took the Grand Tour through Italy, read Cicero and Dante, and studied and revered the monuments, physical and intellectual, of the Roman Empire and the Rinascimento. Although fewer Americans than Englishmen actually made the trip to Italy, Americans were just as appreciative of the culture and civilization of Italy as their English cousins. In fact, the Italian influence in America was possibly even greater than it was in England for the simple fact that the government and social structure of America was created by men who studied Italian and Roman philosophy and political theory. Unlike in the nations of Europe, America's constitution and fundamental laws were created by a group of intellectuals, who were able to take as models what they considered to be the best in European government. Because European thought during the eighteenth century drew so much inspiration from the writers of ancient Rome and the Rinascimento, it is not surprising that Italian philosophy should have had a profound influence on the founding fathers.

One of the Founding Fathers whose philosophy owed a great deal to Italy was Thomas Jefferson. Jefferson was a true eighteenth century scholar, who could read and write Latin and Italian, and who had such a reverence for the philosophers of ancient Rome, he actually used to write them letters. He also struck up a correspondence with an Italian intellectual and dilettante named Filippo Mazzei. Mazzei, on Jefferson's invitation, came to America with the intention of founding an experimental farm in Virginia, where he could introduce Italian vines and seeds. Once in America, however, Mazzei's energies strayed away from agriculture and towards politics. The American Revolution was just beginning to gather force, and Mazzei wrote articles encouraging revolutionary action. His experimental farm was located next to Monticello, Jefferson's home, and Mazzei and Jefferson spent long hours together, discussing forms of government and the anatomy of justice. With Jefferson's encouragement and collaboration, Mazzei continued to write articles and pamphlets, examining the philosophical grounds for the Revolution. Some of the articles which Mazzei wrote and Jefferson translated bear a striking resemblance to passages in Jefferson's Declaration of Independence, both in content and in wording. It was Mazzei, for example, who constantly stressed the importance of the equality of men under the law. In one article, Mazzei wrote "All men are by nature free and independent;" a statement which may have inspired Jefferson's famous "All men are created equal." Whether Mazzei deserves direct credit for Jefferson's philosophy is a matter open to debate. One thing for certain is that the material covered by the Declaration was openly discussed by the two friends: Jefferson even sent one of the first copies of the Declaration, written in his own hand, to Mazzei.

Another contemporary Italian thinker who influenced Jefferson and the other founding fathers was Cesare Beccaria. Born in Milan

[167]

in 1738, Beccaria was an economist and philosopher who wrote tremendously influential articles and pamphlets at a very early age. His most important work, a book called *Dei delitti e delle pene* (translated as *Crimes and Punishments*), was published when he was only twenty six years old. Although the book is ostensibly concerned with the problems of developing a just and effective criminal code, *Crimes and Punishments* also has a great deal to say about the structure of a good and free society. Beccaria puts forth the idea that the best way to prevent crimes is to make sure that laws are clear, just, and understandable, and to realize that the goal of the laws should be to bring about a society in which "the maximum happiness (is) divided among the greatest number of people." The first modern philosopher to examine and denounce the practice of capital punishment, Beccaria also spoke out against torture and secret accusations, while demonstrating that a truly just society respects the liberty of its subjects above anything else. Beccaria was extremely sensitive to subtle forms of tyranny, and because of this, argued convincingly about the necessity of separating church and state, an idea which was quickly adopted by America's Founding Fathers.

Beccaria's book, *Crimes and Punishments*, was immediately recognized as a significant work throughout Europe, and eventually was translated into twenty-two languages. Editions of the book found their way into the hands of the leaders of the American Revolution, most notably Jefferson and John Adams. Jefferson frequently quotes from Beccaria in his writings, and Adams, who was struggling to learn Italian, possessed at least two copies of the book, one in English and one in Italian. He even gave one of his sons an English edition as a present. This book, which Adams filled with hand written notes, can be found in the rare book room of the Boston Public Library.

The philosophy of the Founding Fathers was clearly fertilized by the writings of Italians, as well as by the writings of other European thinkers. The extent of the Italian influence on early American government can never truly be measured. While writers like Mazzei and Beccaria surely helped to crystallize the thoughts of Jefferson, Adams and others, we can never know for certain how much of American philosophy truly springs from an Italian source. The Italian influence on the physical shape of the new American government, however, is more definite and obvious. Once Washington was chosen as the site for the new capital of America, the Founding Fathers wasted no time before calling in Italian experts to build it. Jefferson, whose own home, Monticello, bears an Italian name and was designed following Palladio's classical architectural principles, wrote to Mazzei, who was back in Italy, asking him to round up Italian sculptors, painters and architects to come and lend their skills to Washington. Washington's monuments and official buildings clearly display America's Italian heritage. Not only were many of the edifices built and decorated by Italian hands, the design of the most important buildings in the capitol is specifically classical, recalling not only Palladio and Rinascimento architecture, but the buildings of ancient Rome as well. The Supreme Court building, for instance, is a virtual copy of the *Maison Carrée* in Nîmes, while the Capitol building takes St. Peter's in Rome for its model.

In fact, the city of Washington D. C. owes much of its splendor to Italian artistry. The Capitol, as we know it today, took many decades to complete, and over the years, more and more Italians contributed to its decoration. Most famous among the beautifiers of Washington was a painter named Constantino Brumidi, who came to the United States from Rome in the middle of the nineteenth century. Brumidi, who is often called the "Michelangelo of the United States Capitol," painted frescos on the interior of many of the most important buildings of the city, including the Senate and the House of Representatives Chambers, and the Capitol Rotunda and dome. His work on the circular ceiling of the dome covered 4,664 square feet of concave surface with magnificent scenes from American history. Like Michelangelo, Brumidi did his painting lying flat on his back, suspended one hundred and eighty feet above the Rotunda floor. Brumidi painted prolifically for over a quarter of a century, continuing to cover walls and ceilings with lifelike scenes despite his advancing years. His career ended at the age of seventy-two, when, in completing a fresco on the wall of the Rotunda, he slipped off of the support he had been standing on, and was only saved from falling the fifty-eight feet to the floor by catching hold of a rung of a ladder with one hand. Although he

[169]

was not injured, the shock of the accident apparently shattered his nerve. He did not go back to his painting, and before the year was out, he died.

Although Constantino Brumidi may not have gotten all of the credit that he deserved for his life's work, his name is not forgotten, and a marble bust of him, commissioned by the Senate in 1966, stands in a corridor which he painted in the Senate wing of the Capitol. Many other Italian artists and artisans who contributed their work to America have no such recognition, but from the days of the Revolution until the twentieth century, Italians have been the chief sculptors, monumental painters and stone workers of our country. Especially in the earliest days of our history, Americans relied upon European artists to provide them with statues of their heros and to decorate their buildings. Although many great American sculptures come from France, many are also Italian in origin. Even the Statue of Liberty, which most people know was conceived in France and donated to America by the French people, was sculpted by Auguste Bertholdi, a Frenchman whose father immigrated from Italy. Numerous smaller, less important sculptures and statues in cities throughout the United States were created by Italian artists. Despite the political disarray and the poverty in which the Italian peninsula found itself during the eighteenth and nineteenth centuries, the traditional arts of the Italian people continued to be practiced, and, as a result, Italy could supply the world with a reservoir of talented artisans who learned techniques passed down from Rinascimento masters.

American architects brought Italian art works and Italian craftsmen to the United States because the Italians were the most skilled and best educated artists of the time. However, just because the Americans recognized the superiority of the Italian artist does not mean that Italian craftsmen were always treated as well or paid as handsomely as they ought to have been. Indeed, stories of exploitation of Italian stone masons and builders can be found throughout history. The Italian worker, however, did not always take his mistreatment lying down. A story is told at Yale University about a group of stone workers brought over from Italy to decorate the exteriors of some new, gothic buildings with classical sculpted scenes and reliefs. Mid-way through the job, however, the

Above: *Maison Carée* in Nîmes, France, inspiration for
Below: Supreme Court building in Washington, D.C.

Above: La Rotunda, Vicenza Italy, inspiration for
Below: Thomas Jefferson's Virginia home, Monticello

Italians discovered that they were being underpaid for their work. After discussions with their employers, the Italians realized that they were trapped: either they could finish the job for unsatisfactory pay, or they could quit and have no pay at all. The stone masons decided to finish the job, and for many months they carved their intricate scenes and tiny statues onto the walls of the stately new buildings, taking extreme care over their work - only now what they carved was subtly different. Instead of depicting dignified classical scenes, the workers carved gothic gargoyles: fat demons sticking out their tongues, old ladies exposing their buttocks, children making obscene gestures to passersby. The masons, according to the story, never got the money they deserved, but they did get the last laugh. Today, sharp-eyed visitors to Yale can still see those defiant Italian faces laughing from the walls of the ornate university buildings.

Until the end of the nineteenth century, the number of Italian immigrants to the United States was relatively small. Most of the earliest immigrants were from the north of Italy, and most were from the middle class. They were artists and artisans, musicians and intellectuals, and they frequently earned their living in the United States teaching Italian or music or painting to upper class Americans. Around the middle of the nineteenth century, groups of Italian wine makers began to immigrate to California, where, they quickly discovered, the climate was ideal for growing grapes.

As the nineteenth century progressed, more and more Italians began to see America as the land of opportunity, and the tide of Italian immigration began to rise. By the early years of the twentieth century, Italians were pouring into America; sometimes as many as fifteen thousand of them would arrive on American shores in a single day, seeking work, citizenship, education, and, most importantly, a land where they would have a chance to realize their dreams. In 1870, Italy herself had finally thrown off foreign domination of her territories and unified all Italian lands under one government. The unification of Italy, however, did little for her war-ravaged economy, and many Italians, particularly those in the south, were crushingly poor. There was no work to be had, little pay, no chance for advancement, little if any education for the children, and no room to dream.

[171]

America was a way out; not only could a young man go to America and find work, he could easily earn enough money to send some home to his family. America was still a young and largely wild country which the Americans were desperately trying to tame. America needed workers to build her roads and railways, mine her coal and clear her lands. By the end of the nineteenth century, railway and coal mining companies had developed a system of sending representatives over to Italy to recruit and import young men who wanted to work. Often a man would go to America with the intention of earning some money and coming back to live in Italy, but more frequently than not, he would decide to stay in the new country instead, sometimes returning to Italy for the sole purpose of bringing his family back to America with him, or of collecting his childhood sweetheart and bringing her back as his wife. Although America offered the poor Italian a chance for advancement that would never have been possible in the old country, the work that he had to do was often back-breakingly hard, and, by American standards, poorly paid. Many Italian immigrants worked their whole lives away from morning until night for the sole reward of seeing their children go off to college and rise in the world of business, law, or medicine. Italian immigrants may have profited from the opportunities that America provided, but America was far the richer for the contribution of hard work and loyalty of her Italian citizens.

The tremendous flow of Italians into America was slowed dramatically by the first World War, as well as by new immigration laws which were designed to limit the growth of the immigrant population. Because the majority of Italians who came to America during the early part of the twentieth century were poor and uneducated, many Americans developed a negative stereotype of Italy and of Italian people. Surprising though it may seem in light of Italy's obvious contributions to the advancement of culture, some Americans still see Italy as a backward country full of impoverished, superstitious and ignorant people. Not only do these Americans forget about the tremendous achievements of Italians from the days of Rome and the Rinascimento, they choose to ignore the advances of the numerous Italian scientists and inventors whose experiments and discoveries have made possible today's technological revolution.

Although Italian names do not dominate the roster of scientists who have helped to expand our understanding of the forces of the universe, Italians continue to contribute more than their share to the world of science. Back at the end of the eighteenth century, for instance, a physicist from Como by the name of Alessandro Volta invented the electric battery which provided the first source of continuous current in the world. The "volt" - a measure of electrical potential - was named after him. Volta's friend, Luigi Galvani also experimented with electricity, and the word "galvanize", meaning to stimulate with electric current, is named for him. Not all Italian inventors, however, were as lucky as Volta and Galvani, whose names have become an integral part of the English language. Some have been overlooked or forgotten by the history books.

The most notable example of an inventor who never got the credit (or the financial rewards) he deserved for his invention was an Italian immigrant named Antonio Meucci. The debate still rages on. Was the true inventor of the telephone the modest and impoverished Italian immigrant by the name of Meucci, or was it really Alexander Graham Bell, the well-educated and well-spoken Scottish immigrant who held a professorship at Boston University? Although many people today claim that the real credit for the creation of the telephone ought to go to Meucci, Graham Bell undeniably got both the fame and the profit. Certainly Meucci, among others, made pioneering steps towards inventing a telephone. As early as 1850, he had a prototype of a telephone hooked up in his house, which, using electromagnetic current, could communicate sounds through its copper wires. The *telettrophone*, as he called it, was Meucci's pet project. He worked on it constantly for many years, convinced that he had invented something which would revolutionize communications in the world.

By 1860, Meucci was confident that his invention would bring him fame and fortune, but he could not afford a patent. He continued to perfect the device, meanwhile working on other, smaller projects. Five years later, a description of the still unpatented invention appeared in *L'eco d'Italia*, an Italian language newspaper printed in New York. Meucci was trying to raise money from New

[173]

York Italians. But, sadly, he was destined to fail. During a period of illness not long afterwards, he became so destitute, his wife even sold his only working models of the *telettrophone* to a local junk man for the grand sum of six dollars.

In 1876, Alexander Graham Bell, who had been experimenting with the telephone for two years, obtained a patent for the invention and subsequently displayed it at the World's Fair in Philadelphia, to the applause and admiration of the world. Meucci, who was certain of the priority of his idea, attempted to challenge the Bell patent. A much publicized trial took place, but Bell, armed with MIT engineers as expert witnesses and the superiority of his education, emerged victorious. Meucci, who had lived most of his life in or near to poverty died in 1889, and was buried at the expense of the Italian government.

Meucci was not the only Italian inventor whose energies were directed towards the problems of long range communication. Far more famous and far more successful was the Italian physicist Guglielmo Marconi, who received the Nobel Prize in physics in 1909 for his pioneering work in radio transmissions. Marconi was born in Bologna in 1874, where, at a young age, he began to experiment with electromagnetic waves, which he believed could be used to transmit sounds over distances. Marconi's intuitions proved correct, and it was not long before he could demonstrate a crude form of radio transmission on his father's estate in Pontecchio. When he was in his early twenties, Marconi went to England where he continued his experiments and obtained his first patent for a long range signalling device. He set up his own company, Marconi's Wireless Telegraph Co., and worked at developing the potential for radio transmissions at ever greater distances.

Marconi's inventions attracted considerable publicity in England, Europe and America. His demonstrations, involving long distance communication from England to Europe, as well as from land to ships at sea, aroused world wide excitement about the possibilities of telecommunications. In 1899, he outfitted two ships to monitor and report on the progress of the America's cup yacht race, the first sports broadcast in history. In 1901, he received the first transatlantic message, sent from Cornwall, England, to St. John's, Newfoundland. Later, he sent messages from Ireland to

Argentina and from England to Australia. The world, it seemed, had suddenly become a much smaller and more intimate place. The age of radio communications, broadcasting and navigational services was born.

Not only did Marconi make possible the transmission of messages from one corner of the globe to another, he also made such things as ocean travel far safer. Before the invention of the wireless telegraph, ships which foundered at sea were usually lost: out of sight of land and out of touch with any other living being, people on sinking ships had no choice but to accept their fate. Marconi's radio communications, however, changed the shape of ocean travel. When the famous doomed ship, the *Titanic* struck an iceberg on its maiden voyage in 1912, the ship's telegrapher was able to send the distress call out to another ship, the *Carpathia* which was some sixty miles away and going in the opposite direction. The *Carpathia*, hearing the S.O.S. call, arrived at the location of the now submerged *Titanic*, where sixteen lifeboats held the seven hundred survivors of the disaster. If the *Titanic* disaster had occurred eleven or twelve years earlier, the lifeboats would have been stranded in the ocean: nobody would even know where to begin to look for them. The *Carpathia* carried the survivors to New York Harbor, where they were greeted by none other than Marconi himself, who had heard of the tragedy. The survivors of the *Titanic* were fully aware that they owed their lives to Marconi, and at a thanksgiving ceremony later on, they presented him with a golden plaque to show their thanks.

Marconi's inventions went beyond the sending of sounds from one point to another. He also pioneered work in radio beacons and in radar, filling the airways with invisible guide ropes for airplanes as well as ships. Marconi also was among the scientists of the nineteen thirties who experimented with the use of microwaves to produce heat. Today's microwave oven is a product of microwave research. In earlier decades, microwaves were used experimentally to treat various diseases, a practice known as "Marconi therapy."

While Marconi ushered in the age of radio communications, another Italian helped to bring us to the nuclear age. Enrico Fermi was born in Rome in 1901, and was educated at the University of Pisa. Fermi was tremendously precocious: as a child he read complex books of mathematical physics for pleasure; in college, his professors turned to him for an explanation of Einstein's theory of relativity. While still in his twenties, Fermi, now a professor at the University of Rome, became interested in the atom and in producing controlled nuclear reactions. He lectured in the United States, Argentina and Brazil, and in 1938, received the Nobel Prize in physics for his discoveries concerning artificial radiation. He went to Stockholm with his family to receive the Nobel Prize, but instead of returning to his laboratory in Rome, he and his family escaped to the United States. Italy, in 1938, was under the fascist rule of Benito Mussolini, and Fermi was shocked not only by the militaristic restrictions of the fascist government, but by racial legislation which was then being introduced. Once in America, he took a position at Columbia University and joined a group of scientists who were in the process of studying nuclear energy.

Although Fermi was only one of the many scientists at work in the development of nuclear energy, it was the group under Fermi's leadership which produced the world's first self-sustaining nuclear chain reaction. When an American physicist called a colleague at Harvard to give him the news of Fermi's success, he said "Jim, you will be interested to know that the Italian navigator has landed in the New World." Fermi's work lead to the creation of the atomic bomb, which effectively ended the second World War, and assured the United States, at least for the time being, military superiority over the rest of the world. The ability to create and control nuclear energy has far more beneficial uses than the creation of bombs, however. Nuclear science has the potential to create abundant supplies of clean, useable energy, as well as new therapeutic and diagnostic medical tools. Today, we have yet to solve all of the problems that using nuclear energy poses for us: we are waiting for another Fermi to come up with innovative ways to produce nuclear energy safely and without the production of dangerous radioactive waste.

Not all of America's Italian heroes have been scientists and inventors. Italians have excelled in just about every possible area of American life, from athletic competitions and entertaining to gourmet cooking, politics and business. Most famous among Italian businessmen was Amadeo Giannini, founder of the Bank of Italy,

Enrico Fermi, father of the atomic bomb

A. P. Giannini, Founder, Bank of America

which would later buy out the Bank of America and become one of the largest banking establishments in the world. Giannini was the son of immigrant parents who got his start in business working with his stepfather, a fruit peddlar in the San Francisco Bay area. In 1904, when he was thirty-four years old, he opened his first bank, called the Bank of Italy, which he tailored to the needs of the Italian community. Unlike other banks of the day, the Bank of Italy focussed on the small investor, and freely lent out money to new immigrants, who frequently arrived in America with little more than their bodies and a strong desire to work. The Bank of Italy got off to a good start, but the event that really established it as a major success was the 1906 San Francisco earthquake.

The earthquake itself did not destroy San Francisco; the devastation was caused by the fires which ripped through the city afterwards, many of them fed by broken gas mains. Giannini kept his head during the calamity: he went down to his offices in the North Beach area of the city and, along with his staff, collected the bank's cash reserves, gold and the bank records, and took them back to his home in San Mateo. He then went down to the waterfront and commissioned the captains of ships to sail to the Oregon coast and collect lumber with which to begin rebuilding the burning city. As a result, the North Beach section of San Francisco was the first to recover from the effects of the fire. A few days after the earthquake, most of San Francisco's other banks were closed. Their cash was protected in fireproof underground vaults, but they were still too hot to be opened. Their bank records had been destroyed. The bank holiday lasted for over a month. People who had lost everything in the fire had no way to get at their money.

Except, of course, in the Italian section of town. Within four days of the disaster, the Bank of Italy was open for business. Giannini, who knew most of his depositors personally, set up a makeshift table down on the Washington Street wharf. There he handed out money to his needy customers. If somebody unknown to him came and asked for a loan, he would request to see the man's hands. If the hands had callouses on them, Giannini would give him the money. Giannini believed in hard-working people and they believed in him. Not one of people that he lent money to in that troubled time defaulted on his loan. After the disaster was over, Giannini's bank was flooded with small depositors. Here, finally, was a bank that the people could trust. It was Giannini's lifelong commitment to serving the average people of America which made his bank one of the most successful in the world.

Italian Americans have also distinguished themselves in the political arena. Even back in the eighteenth century, Italian immigrants held publicly elected offices in the United States. Although Italian Americans have yet to send a son to the White House, they came closer than anybody has before to sending a daughter, in the person of Geraldine Ferraro, the first woman ever to be nominated as Vice President on a major party ticket. Italian Americans have served in the Senate and in Congress, and there have been quite a few notable state governors and city mayors of Italian heritage. Perhaps the most noteworthy Italian American mayor from the not-too-distant-past was Fiorello La Guardia of New York, who served as mayor for three terms, from 1933 to 1945, and is still remembered by many as the best mayor New York ever had. La Guardia, like Giannini, never forgot the little people who made up his constituency, and he fought valiantly for their rights, at the same time striving to eradicate the corruption and waste which was choking the New York political system. A man full of fire and passion, La Guardia remained so sensitive to the needs of the people that during a prolonged newspaper strike in the city, he actually used to read the comic pages over the radio, so that children of New York would not be deprived of their daily amusement.

Italians in this country have had a profound effect on many aspects of American life, slowly changing and improving its flavor, nowhere more so than in the area of American cuisine. A half a century ago, most Americans would not know what a pizza was. They considered spaghetti and macaroni foreign dishes. Mozzarella and Parmesan cheeses, as well as olive oil and olives were only available at specialty stores. The pizza, which is a regional dish from Naples, has spread around the world and throughout America. There is scarcely a town in this country in which one cannot obtain a pizza of one kind or another. Spaghetti and other forms of pasta, are one of the most popular dishes among the children of America, and make up a significant portion of today's

American diet. Italian cuisine has infiltrated the kitchens of America, and has now become the trendiest and most fashionable style of cooking in the land. Whereas formerly the only Italian restaurants in this country served hearty southern Italian food, nowadays restaurants serving lighter northern Italian food rival even French restaurants in their expensive chic.

Now that Italian cooking is fashionable, even the most exotic of Italian ingredients can be found in grocery stores in every large city of America. The grocery stores also contain many Italian-made and Italian-owned products, which most people think of as simply American. For instance, how many people realize that the Planter's Peanut company was founded and owned by Amedeo Obici, an Italian immigrant? Chun King brand canned Chinese food was also founded by an Italian American. Italo Marchiony, another Italian immigrant, invented the ice cream cone, and even received a patent for it in 1903.

Although Italian food has established a strong foothold in America, Italian drink has an even more dominant position. California's wine industry, which began back in the middle of the nineteenth century, is largely an Italian American industry. The Gallo winery in Modesto California, run for many years by Julio and Ernest Gallo, sons of an immigrant from Piedmont, is the largest wine producer in the world, having among other things, the world's largest winery, its own bottling factory and the world's largest private wine and grape research laboratory. Under all of its various labels, Gallo sells over one hundred million gallons of wine a year, an amount which comprises a full quarter of all the wine sold in the United States.

Gallo is just one of the many wineries in California that is run by Italian Americans. During the first decade of the twentieth century, many Italian vintners vied for prominence in the California sunshine. Then came Prohibition, and with it, the death knell for a great number of these companies. Some wine growers began to produce table grapes, or other fruits and crops instead of wine. Some hung on, certain that the madness of Prohibition could not last forever. To make ends meet during this period, many companies sold grape juice concentrate, which, when properly diluted and stored, would ferment into wine. One Italian American company which sold the concentrate put a large warning label on the bottle. "Caution," the label read "Do not place the diluted solution in a warm dark place for a long period of time, or the solution will ferment, which is against the law."

Italy today is one of the most popular vacation spots in the world, as well as a mecca for students of art, music, fashion and fine cuisine, not to mention religious pilgrims, historians and archaeologists. From its earliest days, Italy has been a land which has produced great minds, great ideas and great works of art. At the forefront of Western culture, Italy has historically sent out emissaries to foreign countries, bringing higher culture and a higher standard of living to the other nations of the world. When we look at Italy today, we see the land which, more than any other, is responsible for the color and the music in western culture, the land which civilized and tamed the wild world beyond it. Italy is an old country, and a wise one. American tourists, even if they don't go to a museum, and only travel in order to eat good food and to buy trinkets from the street vendors, cannot help but realize that beneath the soil on which they walk lie the very roots of their culture.

In America we have no Roman ruins to remind us of our connection to the ancient peoples of Italy, but our culture is founded upon theirs nonetheless. Not only do many of our laws and social customs descend directly from Roman society, but our whole concept of how the world should operate comes from Roman times. We want to foster a new world peace, a new pax romana which will ensure the happiness and the safety of our children and of our children's children. We believe, like the Romans, that peace comes from military strength and just leaders in a society governed by laws rather than by men. It has often been said that the Americans are the new Romans, and indeed, we probably see ourselves in much the same way as the Romans saw themselves during the height of the Empire. Like the Romans, we Americans are superb road builders and communicators. Like the Romans, we accept talented people of all nationalities into our society and embrace them as Americans. We see ourselves as the newest guardians of Western culture, the leaders of the free world and the most enlightened society on earth. Like the Romans too, we sometimes forget that much of the greatness of our society comes from the contributions of cultures older than our own.

We owe a tremendous debt to the Roman Empire not simply for the ideas and the laws that it has given us, but for the religious and moral sentiments that it spread as well. Indeed, we owe Christianity and all of the culture, art and music that Christianity brought with it, to the Romans who adopted it as their law and helped it to spread to the farthest corners of the earth. Christian moral teachings are at the base of many great American institutions, and the stories and words from Christian scripture lie at the back of much of the great art and literature that the world has produced. Christianity gave us, moreover, a world-wide cultural continuity and a language of symbols which can be understood by people from different countries and different backgrounds. Christians from Italy belong to a culture which is radically different from that of Christians in remote Pacific Islands, and yet, because of the continuity of their religion, they have principles, ideas and sentiments in common. The success of Christianity in uniting such different peoples under a single religion can be attributed to the fact that the Roman Empire lent Christianity its tremendously efficient organization.

America is indebted to Italy in so many ways it becomes hard to count them. Perhaps most of all, America is indebted to the Italians of the Rinascimento, who not only discovered and named her, but who provided the humanist philosophy and the spirit of inquiry into the nature of justice and liberty which forged the newest and the bravest nation on earth. The founders of our America followed the lead of their Italian Rinascimento forefathers, looking back into the past and attempting to revive the best of ancient Rome. The Rinascimento was the beginning of the modern world, and the source of inspiration for artists, scientists and musicians the world over. The Italians of the Rinascimento started an intellectual and artistic movement which is even now affecting the way we look at the world.

Over the past two thousand years, Italians have proven themselves the cultural, and sometimes political leaders of the world. Three great forces have come out of the Italian peninsula; first the Romans, then the Christians, and, finally the Rinascimento humanists. Each of these three forces inspired the world to look to Italy for guidance. In addition to these major Italian movements, major cultural disciplines, such as music and sculpture have always considered Italy their home. Italians, both at home and abroad, have always been among the most prolific contributors to the advancement of the human condition. Just because Italy's past is filled with greatness, there is no reason to suppose that Italy's greatness is in the past. Indeed, even today it seems that Italy is on the verge of pulling herself out of the economic and political chaos that has engulfed her ever since the days of the Rinascimento. With a recovering economy, and a surge of business, not to mention a new, world wide awareness of the charms of Italian culture, who is to say that we are not about to experience a fourth great Italian force which will fundamentally change and improve the way we look at the world?

Geraldine Ferraro, discussing her Congressional Campaign with President Carter
Washington, D.C. , 1978

Italian immigrants to America

Epilogue

We might well ask what this world would be like if it were not for the contributions of Italy and her children. Take away the Italian elements of our society, and what is left? It would be impossible to speculate. Not only have the Italians contributed more than their share to the fabric of our society, they are central to its very composition. From the dawn of Western Civilization, Italy has provided leadership, organization, brilliance and inspiration to every society she has come in contact with. Without the influence of Italy, the only certain thing about our world is that it would be an immeasurably poorer place.

What, for instance, could be expected from a world which never benefitted from the tremendous presence of the Roman Empire? The Romans not only conquered Europe, they civilized it. They brought running water, monuments, schools and libraries into the virtual jungles of primitive European society. They introduced the concepts of city planning, organized government, standardized coinage and established laws to backward, tribal groups. Great Roman thinkers and writers expanded the limits of the human mind while great Roman generals and statesmen extended the scope of the Empire itself. The Romans brought peace, order and learning to the entire western world and laid the foundations for all of the many different societies which would later spring up in ancient Roman lands.

The Roman influence lived on after the end of the Roman Empire in many different ways. Perhaps the most important extension of the Empire was the Christianizing of Europe. Without the Romans, who is to say what the state of religion would be in today's world? Without the conversion of Constantine, we might not be living in a Christian world at all. After three hundred years of fighting against Christianity, the Romans finally embraced it in such a way as to ensure its success everywhere. Ten million people were subjects of Rome when Christianity was declared the official state religion. Ten million people were then required by law to declare themselves Christians. From that moment forward, our world was formed by Christian thinking.

While the teachings of Christ might well have prevailed even without the help of the Romans, it was the Roman Empire which gave Christianity its organization. Without the Romans, not only would Christianity have had to fight its way into many different cultures, it would have had to do so without a universal language that everybody could understand, and without an underlying structure. Christianity marched across Europe on the roads built by Rome, both literally and figuratively. Not only did the Roman Empire make it easier for Christianity to dominate Europe, Rome itself became the center of the Christian world. The city became a holy city, and pilgrims from near and far came to Italy for religious enlightenment. Even though Italy itself was politically fragmented during the Middle Ages, Rome remained the most important city in Europe.

Although the Roman Empire and Christianity are two great gifts from Italy, the third gift, the Rinascimento, was perhaps the greatest of all. The Rinascimento combined the enlightenment and learning of the Romans, the spirituality of the Christians and the natural joyous creativity of Italy to produce one of the most fruit-ful, artistic and exciting periods in human history. The great painters, sculptors, architects and writers of the Rinascimento have never been equalled or even challenged. During the Rinascimento, Italy brought forth more intellectual, artistic and creative giants than any country ever has before or since. Not only did Rinasci-mento Italy give us a tremendous number of geniuses, the Italian humanist movement inspired people from other countries and showed the whole western world new ways of seeing.

The advances of the Rinascimento were not limited to the worlds of art and literature. Italian universities taught astronomy, mathematics, law and medicine to students from every Western

[184]

country. Such great men as Galileo brought about revolutions in the world of science, while such brave explorers as Columbus set out westward to discover new continents. Columbus is such a towering figure in our history that other countries, such as Spain, have tried to claim him for their own, but the fact remains that Columbus was an Italian born in Genoa. Although other European countries sponsored most of the explorations of the New World, Italian navigators were at the helm of practically every major American exploration. Even the head of England's first great expedition, John Cabot, was really an Italian. We all should know him by his real name: Giovanni Cabotto.

The great advances of the Rinascimento ensured that Italy remained the most highly cultured and civilized place in Europe even though the country itself was dominated by foreign powers and torn by war. Well into the eighteenth and nineteenth centuries, Italy was the land of inspiration for countless people: not just artists, writers and architects, but scientists, politicians and lawmakers. Many other European countries owe Italian culture a great debt. France, for instance, developed her highly cultivated and refined society under the influence of Italian born leaders such as Caterina dei Medici. England, as we know it today, was shaped by Italian ideas and images brought back with the luggage of the Grand Tourists. Even the English countryside was remade in the image of Italy.

Where would we be without the Italians? What would the quality of life be without their countless contributions? Nowhere, perhaps, would we feel the loss as deeply as in the world of music. It was an Italian, Guido d'Arezzo, who invented the musical scale which made it possible for music to be recorded precisely, and from that point on, the art of musical composition soared to heights never before attained. Italy gave us as many great composers as she gave us artists, and Italy's music brought new inspiration to composers from all of the countries of Europe. Not only did Italy give us some of the greatest musicians of all time, she also gave us almost all of our most important musical instruments. Imagine a symphony without violins, cellos, and pianos and you will begin to see how poor the musical world would be without the Italian contribution. Now take away the great Italian musical forms, such as the opera, and the great Italian composers such as Verdi and the great Italian performers such as Caruso and Pavarotti. Without the Italian influence, who can say whether we would even have any classical music at all?

We Americans should be particularly proud of the Italian roots of our country. America was discovered by Italians, explored by Italians, and in a large part built by Italians. Why, then, does the average American seem to think of Italy as a backward place? Why is the average Italian American defensive of his heritage instead of proud of it? In a sense, we are victims of our educations, and perhaps, even, of American national pride. America is a great country, but still a young one. Compared to Italy, America, only discovered five hundred years ago, is still in her infancy. Like any child, struggling for identity, perhaps America wants to make light of what she owes to her Italian parent. For three thousand years, Italy has been the cultural leader of the western world, and she is not about to stop now.

Over the centuries, millions of words have been written about Italy. Every aspect of Italian culture has been explored and analyzed, every facet of Italian politics and history has been examined and critiqued, every beautiful landscape and building has been described and praised. The one thing lacking in all of the books that I have ever read or seen is a true perspective on the greatness of Italy's contribution to our world from the beginnings of history up to the present day. Students of art, music or literature may learn about Italy's leadership in their fields without realizing that Italy's influence has also extended into practically every other aspect of their lives. I even know lawyers who will quote legal terms in Latin without taking account of the fact that it was the Romans who gave them their legal principles as well as their legal vocabulary. This lack of perspective on Italy is what prompted me to add these few thousand words to the millions upon millions which already exist praising the great achievements of the Italian people.

Why is having a better perspective on Italy so important? It is not simply so that those of us who have Italian ancestry can be proud of our heritage, nor is it so that people who do not have Italian roots will treat those of us who do with respect and reverence. Learning about our past is the key to understanding our present and controlling our future. One if Rome's greatest writers and orators, Marcus Tullius Cicero, put it best when he said "Not to know what happened before we were born is to remain perpetually a child, for what is the worth of human life unless it is woven into the life of our ancestors by the records of history?"1

Bibliography

Abel, Dominick. *Guide to the Wines of the United States.* New York: Cornerstone Library, 1979.

Adams, Leon D. *The Wines of America.* New York: Mcgraw-Hill, 1985.

Amfitheatrof, Erik. *The Children of Columbus.* Boston: Little, Brown & Co., 1973.

Andreae, Bernard. *The Art Of Rome.* New York: Harry N. Abrams Inc., 1973.

Argan, Giulio Carlo. *The Europe of the Capitals.* Geneva: Editions d'Art Albert Skira, 1964.

Aries, Philippe, and Duby, Georges. *The History of Private Life, From Pagan Rome to Byzantium.* Cambridge: Harvard University Press, 1987.

Arnold, C.J. *Roman Britain to Saxon England.* London: Croom Helm, 1984.

Balsdon, J.P.V.D. *Romans and Aliens.* London: Duckworth, 1979.

Batterberry, Michael. *Art of the Middle Ages.* New York: McGraw Hill, 1971.

Bartoccini, Renato, *The Etruscan Paintings of Tarquinia.* Milan: Aldo Martello Editore, 1973.

Barzini, Luigi. *The Italians.* New York: Atheneum, 1979.

Beccaria, Cesare, *An Essay on Crimes and Punishments.* Brookline: Branden Press, 1983.

Beckford, William. *Italy, Spain and Portugal.* New York; Wiley and Putnam, 1845.

Bonfante, Larissa. *Etruscan Life and Afterlife.* Detroit: Wayne State University Press, 1986.

Bovini, Giuseppe. *Ravenna Mosaics.* New York: E.P. Dutton, 1978.

Brion, Marcel. *The Medici.* New York: Crown Publishers, 1969.

Coats, Peter. *Great Gardens of Britain*. New York: William Morrow & Company, Inc., 1977.

Cartocci, Sergio. *Tivoli*. Rome: Kosmo Publishers, 1979.

Caso, Adolph. *America's Italian Founding Fathers*. Boston: Branden Press, 1975.

Caso, Adolph. *They Too Made America Great*. Boston: Branden Press, 1978.

Clark, Kenneth. *Civilisation*. New York: Harper and Row, 1969.

Clayton, Peter. *A Companion To Roman Britain*. London: Phaidon Press, 1980.

Clifton-Taylor, Alec. *The Cathedrals of England*. London: Thames and Hudson, 1967.

Collis, John Stewart. *Christopher Columbus*. New York: Stein and Day, 1976.

Cornell, Tim and Matthews, John. *Atlas of the Roman World*. New York: Facts on File Inc., 1986.

Crofton, Ian, and Fraser, Donald. *A Dictionary of Musical Quotations*. New York: Schirmer Books, 1985.

Duby, Georges. *The Europe of The Cathedrals*. Geneva: Editions d'Art Albert Skira, 1966.

Embleton, Ronald, and Graham, Frank. *Hadrian's Wall in the Days of the Romans*. Newcastle upon Tyne: Howe Brothers, Ltd., 1984.

Erim, Kenan T.. *Aphrodisias: City of Venus Aphrodite*. London: Muller Blond & White Ltd., 1986.

Fox, David Scott. *Mediterranean Heritage*. Boston: Routledge and Kegan Paul, 1978.

Fox, Robin Lane. *Pagans and Christians*. New York: Alfred A. Knopf, Inc., 1987.

Frend, W.H.C. *The Rise of Christianity*. London: Darton, Longman and Todd, 1984.

Gambini, Yvette. *Nimes Pont du Gard*. Florence: Casa Editriche Bonechi, 1987.

Goldscheider, Ludwig. *Leonardo Da Vinci*. New York: Garden City Books, 1954.

Grant, Michael. *The Art and Life of Pompei and Herculaneum*. Verona: Newsweek Inc., 1979.

Grant, Michael. *The Etruscans*. London: Weidenfeld and Nicolson, 1980.

Grant, Michael. *Roman Myths*. New York: Dorset Press, 1984.

Grant, Robert M. *Early Christianity and Society*. Harper and Row: San Francisco, 1977.

Granzotto, Gianni. Christopher Columbus: *The Dream and the Obsession*. New York: Doubleday and Co., 1985.

Grout, Donald Jay. *A History of Western Music.* New York: W. W. Norton & Co., 1980.

Hadas, Moses. *Imperial Rome.* New York: Time Inc., 1965.

Hale, John R.. *Renaissance.* New York: Time Inc., 1965.

Hamblin, Dora Jane. *The Etruscans.* London: Time-Life International., 1979.

Hamilton, Olive. *Paradise of Exiles.* London: Andre Deutsch. 1974.

Hanson, Richard P.C.. *Studies in Christian Antiquity.* Edinburgh: T.& T. Clark LTD, 1985.

Hay, Denys. *The Age of The Renaissance.* New York: McGraw-Hill Book Co., 1968.

Hay, Denys. *The Medieval Centuries.* New York: Harper and Row, 1964.

Held, Julius, and Posner, David. *17th and 18th Century Art.* New York: Harry Abrams, Inc.

Howard, Clare. *English Travellers of the Renaissance.* New York: John Lane Company, 1913.

Hunt, E.D. *Holy Pilgrimage in the Later Roman Empire.* New York: Oxford University Press, 1982.

Jacobs, Arthur. *A Short History Of Western Music.* New York: Drake Publishers, 1973.

Jackson-Stops, Gervase and Pipkin, James. *The English Country House: A Grand Tour.* Boston: Little, Brown & Co. 1985.

Johnson, Paul. *A History of Christianity.* New York: Atheneum, 1976.

Johnston, William M.. *In Search of Italy.* University Park: Pennsylvania State University Press, 1987.

Keats, John. *The New Romans.* New York: J. B. Lippincott Company, 1965.

Keaveney, Arthur. *Rome and The Unification of Italy.* London:Croom Helm, 1987.

Kirchner, *Western Civilization.* New York: Barnes & Noble, Inc. 1960.

Krautheimer, Richard. *Three Christan Capitals.* Los Angeles: University of California Press, 1982.

Kupferberg, *A History of Opera.* New York: Newsweek Books, 1975.

Lacey, W.K., *Cicero and the End of the Roman Republic.* London, 1978.

Landels, J.G. *Engineering in the Ancient World.* Los Angeles: University of California Press, 1978.

Lazenby, J. F. *Hannibal's War.* Warminster: Aris & Phillips, 1978.

Massa, Aldo, (Anthony Werner, trans.) *The World of the Etruscans.* New York: Tudor Publishing, 1973.

McEvedy, Colin. *The Penguin Atlas of Medieval History.* Baltimore: Penguin Books, 1961.

Macnamara, Ellen. *Everyday Life of The Etruscans.* New York: J.P. Putnams' Sons, 1973.

[191]

Mead, William Edward. *The Grand Tour in the Eighteenth Century.* Boston: Houghton Mifflin Company. 1914.

Mezzanotte, Riccardo (editor). *The Simon and Schuster Book Of The Opera* New York: Simon and Schuster, 1978.

Miller, Hugh M. *History of Music.* New York: Barnes & Noble, Inc., 1953.

Moquin, Wayne. *A Documentary History of the Italian Americans.* New York: Praeger Publishers, 1974.

Musmanno, Michael A., *The Story of The Italians in America.* Garden City: Doubleday & Company, 1965.

Norwich, John Julius. *The Italians: History, Art, and the Genius of a People.* New York: Harry Abrams, Inc., 1983.

Pagels, Elaine. *Adam, Eve, and The Serpent.* New York: Random   House, 1988.

Pallottino, Massimo. *The Etruscans.* Bloomington: Indiana University Press, 1975.

Pierik, Marie. *The Spirit of Gregorian Chant.* Boston: Bruce Humphries Publishers, 1939.

Pirenne, Henri. *Mohammed and Charlemagne.* London: George Allen and Unwin, 1965.

Pleasants, Henry. *The Great Singers.* New York: Simon & Schuster, 1966.

Plumb, J.H.. *The Renaissance.* New York: Doubleday & Co., 1961.

Pollit, J.J.. *The Art of Rome.* Englewood Cliffs: Prentice-Hall, Inc., 1966.

Richardson, A.E.. *Georgian Architecture.* New York: Pellegrini & Cudahy.

Rodin, Auguste. *Cathedrals of France.* trans. Elisabeth Geissbuhler. Boston: Beacon Press, 1965.

Rosenstiel, Leonie. *Schirmer History of Music.* New York: Schirmer, 1982.

Salvadori, Massimo. *A Pictorial History of The Italian People.* New York: Crown Publishers, 1972.

Samachson, Dorothy & Joseph. *The Fabulous World of Opera.* New York: Rand McNally & Co., 1962.

Seznec, Jean. *The Survival of the Pagan Gods.* New York: Harper and Row, 1961.

Shepherd, Massey H.. "Before and After Constantine." from *The Impact of the Church Upon Its Culture.* Chicago: University of Chicago Press, 1968.

Sitwell, N.H.H. *Roman Roads of Europe.* New York: St. Martin's Press, 1981.

Snyder, James. *Medieval Art.* New York: Harry Abrams, Inc., 1989.

Sprenger, Maja. *The Etruscans.* New York: Harry Abrams, Inc., 1983.

Stokstad, Marilyn. *Medieval Art.* New York: Harper & Row, 1986.

Stierlin, Henri. *Le Monde de Rome*. Paris: Editions Princesse, 1982.

Trease, Geoffrey. *The Grand Tour*. London: William Heinemann Ltd. 1967.

Vasari, Giorgio. (Edmund Fuller ed.) *Lives of the Painters, Sculptors and Architects*. New York: Dell Publishing, 1968.

von Cles-Reden, Sibylle (C.M. Woodhouse trans.) *The Buried People*. New York: Charles Scribner's Sons, 1955.

von Simson, Otto. *The Gothic Cathedral*. New York: Harper and Row, 1962.

Vitruvius. *The Ten Books on Architecture*. New York: Dover Publications, 1960.

Wardman, Alan. *Religion and Statecraft Among the Romans*. Baltimore: Johns Hopkins University Press, 1982.

Wechsberg, Joseph. *The Glory of the Violin*. New York: Viking Press, 1973.

Werner, Paul. *Life In Rome In Ancient Times*. Geneva: Editions Minerva, 1978.

Wheeler, Sir Mortimer. *Roman Art and Architecture*. New York: Frederick Praeger, Publishers, 1964.

Wright, Thomas. *Caricature History Of The Georges*. London: John Camden Hotten, 1868.

About The Authors

CARL A. PESCOSOLIDO, who grew up in Italian family in Newton, Massachusetts, is a graduate of Harvard College and a fervent supporter of education and the arts. A talented sprinter and football player, he is well known at Harvard as holder of the record for the longest runback of a kickoff in the Harvard Stadium, established in 1932 against Dartmouth College. In his career as a highly successful entrepreneur and businessman, he owned and operated one of New England's largest independent oil companies before his retirement in 1988. Three of his sons and five of his grandchildren have followed his footsteps to Harvard, where he has endowed a chair in the Classics in order to further the study and appreciation of our Italian ancestors.

PAMELA GLEASON was born in Cambridge, Massachusetts to a distinguished academic family. She is a 1983 *summa cum laude* graduate of Yale, holds a Master's Degree in French literature from New York University, and speaks both French and Italian. Her father's grandfather was a Swiss-Italian who came to America at the turn of the century and established a vineyard in California.